Active LEARNING
Curriculum for Excellence

Fourth Level

HOME ECONOMICS

Edna Hepburn and Lynn Smith

Text © Edna Hepburn and Lynn Smith
Design and layout © 2012 Leckie
Cover image © Eduardo Iturralde

02/051112

ISBN 978-1-84372-819-1

Published by
Leckie
An imprint of HarperCollins*Publishers*
Westerhill Road, Bishopbriggs, Glasgow, G64 2QT
T: 0844 576 8126 F: 0844 576 8131
leckiescotland@harpercollins.co.uk   www.leckiescotland.co.uk

HarperCollins *Publishers*
Macken House, 39/40 Mayor Street Upper, Dublin 1, D01 C9W8, Ireland

Special thanks to
Planman (page layout and creative packaging)
Jill Laidlaw (copy-editor), Donna Cole (proofreader)
Roda Morrison (proofreader), Eduardo Iturralde (illustrator)

A CIP Catalogue record for this book is available from the British Library.

Acknowledgements
Leckie has made every effort to trace all copyright holders.
If any have been inadvertently overlooked, we will be pleased to make the necessary arrangements.

Printed in the United Kingdom.

MIX
Paper | Supporting
responsible forestry
FSC™ C007454

This book is produced from independently certified FSC™ paper
to ensure responsible forest management.

For more information visit: www.harpercollins.co.uk/green

CONTENTS

CONTENTS

HOW TO USE THIS BOOK

Leckie & Leckie's Active Learning series has been developed specifically to provide teachers, students and parents with the ability to implement Curriculum for Excellence as effectively as possible. Each book has been written with the following objectives in mind:
- To support the implementation of Curriculum for Excellence in schools.
- To engage students by taking a contextualised learning approach and providing a range of rich task activities.
- To assist teachers with the planning and delivery of lessons and assessment.

COVERING CURRICULUM FOR EXCELLENCE

Active Home Economics comprehensively covers the Fourth Level Outcomes and Experiences for *Home Economics*.

The Experiences and Outcomes have been organised into chapters, with a different topic covered on each double-page spread. Please see pages 8–10 for more information on the Experiences and Outcomes covered in this book.

On each spread, key topic knowledge is enhanced by a practical example, illustration or case-study to reinforce learning. A *Top Tip* is also included to highlight key information.

ADDRESSING THE PRIORITIES OF CURRICULUM FOR EXCELLENCE

Active Home Economics focuses on methods to implement the philosophy underpinning Curriculum for Excellence. It addresses Curriculum for Excellence in a thoroughly practical way that makes learning both engaging and fun!
- Ideas for rich task activities are provided for every topic to enable pupils to gain experiences as well as learning outcomes.
- Paired and group learning activities encourage students to take responsibility for and direct their own learning, while developing the four capacities.
- Creative ideas are offered for making cross-disciplinary links with other classroom subjects, within the Technologies and Health and Wellbeing faculties and, more widely, to help ensure students join up their learning.
- The relevance of each topic to everyday life is highlighted in order to help students transfer their skills and knowledge to other areas of their lives.

The toolkit of ideas, subject links and activities contained in *Active Home Economics* can be used in the classroom and/or at home. Please see pages 5–7 for details of the text design and key features of the book.

Each double-page spread includes the following features:

 ACTIVITIES page. This page contains questions and rich tasks to deepen understanding of each topic.

 MAKE THE LINK box. This box highlights the relevance of the topic to a number of other school subjects. This enables learners to gain a more holistic understanding of each topic.

 OUR EVERYDAY LIVES box. This box provides an example of how each topic relates to real life, in order to demonstrate its practical relevance.

DID YOU KNOW? box. This box contains an additional fact about each topic to engage further interest and to bring the subject to life. It can also be used as an extension activity to broaden and deepen learning.

END OF UNIT FEATURES

At the end of each unit, *Active Home Economics* has the following features that encourage deeper exploration of the topic and provide the means for self- and peer-assessment:

 **INTERDISCIPLINARY PROJECT** Rich task activities around each unit to bring learning to life; ideas for interdisciplinary project work.

ACTIVITIES Further activity-based tasks, for individual, paired, or group exploration.

 **PERSONAL REVIEW** A section that encourages students to reflect on what they have learned in the course of the unit, including:

 A learning checklist to help students assess and improve their own progress.

 THINK-PAIR-SHARE An opportunity to record and share, through discussed and written self- and peer-assesment, the main learning points of the unit.

KEY FEATURES

Each double page spread contains the following features (see below). In addition, at the end of each unit, there are even more activities as well as tools to help track progress.

KEY WORDS
Most important words and phrases highlighted in bold

FULL COLOUR
Bright and stimulating colour throughout

EXAMPLES
Examples given are captivating and spark students' interest

TOP TIP
Key facts and concepts are highlighted to aid knowledge retention

---

BEAT THE 'G' TEAM ∗ BEAT THE 'G' TEAM

THE 'G' TEAM

The biggest enemies in any food preparation area are food-poisoning bacteria (germs). Bacteria are found everywhere; in the air, on food, on you and on everything you touch. They are microscopic, which means that you cannot see them without a microscope and that's why food covered in bacteria can look and taste normal when you eat it. If you eat foods that contain **pathogenic** (harmful) bacteria, you may develop food poisoning.

Simple personal hygiene and kitchen hygiene rules can help prevent food poisoning.

THE MOST COMMON BACTERIA

Sam
Samonella, found in: raw meat, poultry, raw eggs, unwashed fresh vegetables/herbs, pets, flies, rats and mice.

Eddy
E.coli, found in: human and animal guts. E. coli can be transferred to the meat during slaughter, and can be found in raw meat, unwashed vegetables and water. The real nasty of the G team is E. coli 0157 as it can cause potentially fatal food poisoning.

Susie
Staphylococcus aureus, found in: your nose, hair, mouth, skin, boils and cuts, prepared foods, e.g. cooked meats, poultry and foods that are handled and prepared without further cooking. This is why your own standard of personal hygiene is so important.

THE **G** germ TEAM

Lucy
Listeria, found in: soft cheeses, paté, cook-chill meals, salads and vegetables. This bacteria multiplies even in the low temperature of the fridge. it is important to check 'use-by' dates so that you do not get food poisoning.

Chloe
Campylobacter, found in: raw poultry and meat, milk and animals. This type of bacteria is the most common cause of food poisoning.

Another supporting member of the 'G' team is **Bacillus Cereus**. The easy way to remember which foods it is found in is to link the word 'Cereus' to cereals. This bacteria is found in cooked rice. Ideally you should not reheat left-over rice as this type of bacteria may not be killed. Boil rice in small quantities and serve as soon as possible. It is best to throw out any left-over rice as cooled cooked rice is a high-risk food.

EXAMPLE
The 'G' team needs the following conditions to survive and reproduce.

temperature food moisture time oxygen ph level

To beat the 'G' team you need to break the links of this chain by, for example, keeping foods out of the danger zone. This means storing food at the correct temperature.

TOP TIP

Remember if in doubt, throw it out

22

ACTIVITES TO TRY
Short and engaging revision questions and rich tasks

MAKE THE LINK
draws out links between subjects on a particular topic to aid Interdisciplinary learning and deepen understanding

ACTIVITIES

TASK 1
With a partner, investigate the following:
1. The benefits of good food hygiene practices to food outlets.
2. The groups of people most at risk from food poisoning.
3. The common symptoms of food poisoning.
4. Information about two of the bacteria listed on page 22.

TASK 2
With a partner, write a reply to the following problems about hygiene on the 'Bug Busters' blog.

Dear Bug Busters
We have two pets, a dog and a cat. How can I make sure that they do not spread germs to our food?
Ida Fleas

Dear Bug Busters
I work in a hospital kitchen and have been suffering from a sore stomach and diarrhoea. What should I do?
Di Rhea

Dear Bug Busters
Why must I have my hair tied back and wear a clean apron when working in the kitchen?
Gerty Grott

Dear Bug Busters
I work in a local biscuit factory. Why do I need to wear a blue waterproof plaster over any cuts or sores on my hands?
Nieda Plaster

Dear Bug Busters
My teacher has told me I am not allowed to cook if I have long nails or wear nail varnish. Why?
Miss Vanity

Dear Bug Busters
I have got a few plates and bowls that are chipped. Can I still use them in the kitchen?
Sid Gremlin

TASK 3
Beware of the bugs that are lurking in the kitchen. Design a **Bug Buster Watch** window sticker for the kitchen.

MAKE THE LINK

Science – looking at different types of bacteria.

English – letter writing and completing observation record sheets.

DID YOU KNOW?

Not all bacteria are harmful and some can be useful in cheese and yogurt making. Swiss and Emmental cheeses are made using a type of bacteria that produces carbon dioxide gas bubbles during ageing, giving them their distinctive holes. Bacteria are also essential to the production of yogurt because their role is to spoil and ferment large quantities of milk and turn it into yogurt.

DID YOU KNOW?
boxes provide interesting and engaging facts about each topic to help build knowledge

23

OUR EVERYDAY LIVES

In the supermarket there are many yogurts called 'probiotic' yogurts. Probiotics, a term meaning 'for life', are living bacteria and micro-organisms that may have health benefits, such as helping the immune system stay healthy, protecting against other bacteria that could cause harm to the body, and helping digestion.

OUR EVERYDAY LIVES
Illustrates how the knowledge translates into practical examples drawn from real life

7

Topics	Experiences & Outcomes	TCH 4-10a	TCH 4-10b	TCH 4-11a	TCH 4-11b	TCH 4-11c	TCH 4-11d
		I can confidently apply preparation techniques and processes to make items using specialist skills, materials, equipment or software in my place of learning, at home or in the world of work.	I can explore the properties and functionality of ingredients, materials, equipment or software to establish their suitability for a task at home or in the world of work.	Showing creativity and innovation, I can design, plan and produce increasingly complex food or textile items which satisfy the needs of the user, at home or in the world of work.	I can apply skills of critical thinking when evaluating the quality and effectiveness of my own or others' products.	By examining and discussing the features of everyday products used within the home, I am gaining an awareness of the factors influencing design and can evaluate how these products meet the needs of the user.	Having gained knowledge of colour theory, I can apply it to a food or textile item or when using computer aided design/computer aided manufacture.
The smart cook							
All in the process							
Beat the 'G' team							
Getting it right							
Getting it right for all							
Packaging matters							
Textiles and you							
ABC of Design							

Green indicates good coverage

Yellow indicates a lesser coverage

COVERAGE OF EXPERIENCES AND OUTCOMES

Topics	Experiences & Outcomes	HWB 4-29a	HWB 4-30a	HWB 4-31a	HWB 4-32a	HWB 4-32b
		I enjoy eating a diversity of foods in a range of social situations.	Having researched food and health policy, and dietary legislation, I can explain how this impacts on individuals, the community and the world of work.	I can apply my knowledge and understanding of nutrition, current healthy eating advice and the needs of different groups in the community when planning, choosing, cooking and evaluating dishes.	Having identified diet-related conditions, I can adapt and cook recipes to suit individual needs.	Having assessed how lifestyle or life stages can impact on people's nutritional needs, I can explain how these needs are met.
The smart cook						
All in the process						
Beat the 'G' team						
Getting it right						
Getting it right for all						
Packaging matters						
Textiles and you						
ABC of Design						

Green indicates a good coverage **Yellow** indicates a lesser coverage

Topics	Experiences & Outcomes	HWB 4-33a	HWB 4-34a	HWB 4-35a	HWB 4-36a	HWB 4-37a	HWB 4-37b
		Having explored the conditions for bacterial growth, I can use this knowledge to inform my practice and control food safety risks.	Having explored a range of issues which may affect food choice, I can discuss how this could impact on the individual's health.	Having investigated the effects of food processing on the nutritional value of foods, I can critically assess the place of processed foods in a healthy balanced diet.	I have examined and evaluated food packaging and can understand the legal requirements for manufacturers.	By investigating different influences on the consumer, I can discuss how consumers can be influenced by external sources.	I can explain basic legal rights and responsibilities of the consumer, recognising the agencies that can help.
The smart cook							
All in the process				●			
Beat the 'G' team		●				●	
Getting it right			●				●
Getting it right for all			●				
Packaging matters					●		
Textiles and you							
ABC of Design							

10

LET'S COOK

Food preparation techniques are the key to preparing food. Some techniques you will use on a regular basis while others you will use occasionally.

> Peel, cut, slice, grate, rub in, mix, whisk, cream, blend, roll out, shape.

BASIC TECHNIQUES

Once you have mastered the basic techniques of food preparation you can progress to more complex techniques.

More complex techniques	Description	Foods	Equipment required
Fold	To combine a whisked or creamed mixture with other ingredients without losing any of the air.	Whipped cream, whisked egg white, whisked egg and sugar mixture	Bowl, tablespoon or spatula
Line	To cover the bottom and sides of a flan case with pastry or crushed biscuits.	Pastry, crushed biscuits	Baking tin, rolling pin
Bake blind	To bake a pastry case without a filling.	Pastry	Baking tin, greaseproof paper, tin foil, baking beans
Knead	To handle a pastry or dough to remove cracks before rolling out or shaping.	Bread mix, scone mix, pastry mix	Floured board/work surface, flour dredger
Pipe	To create a shape by forcing a smooth mixture through a nozzle fitted into the end of a piping bag.	Whipped cream, meringue, icing, cake mixture, potatoes	Piping bag and nozzle
Purée	To remove any lumps in food to give a smooth texture.	Soups, sauces, fruits	Blender, sieve
Coat	To cover the outside of a food in a smooth paste or breadcrumb mixture.	Batter, breadcrumbs, chocolate, icing	Bowl, plate
Dice	To cut food into small even-sized cubes.	Fruit, vegetables	Chopping board, cook's knife

As you become more confident in the kitchen you will start attempting more complicated recipes that involve more precise cuts of vegetables such as macédoine, jardinière and paysanne.

EXAMPLE

Knead pastry and biscuit dough gently and for a short time to prevent it becoming stretched and tough when cooked. When kneading bread, use the heel of the hand to pummel the dough with force. This will develop a stretchy substance called **gluten** in the dough and will help it to rise and hold its shape.

ACTIVITIES

TASK 1

Working with a partner and using the resources available:

- Give a brief description of each **basic** technique listed in the think bubble on page 14.
- Make a list of the equipment you could use to carry out each technique.

Your local community centre is setting up a Saturday Cook Club for children in the area. Use the information to make up a set of easy-to-follow cookery cards for the cook club to use with the children. You may wish to use illustrations.

TASK 2

With a partner, find out the size and shape of each of the following different cuts of vegetables:

- macédoine
- jardinière
- paysanne

Working on your own, use the information you have found to make up a recipe bookmark for yourself.

TASK 3

On your own, use magazines or the internet to find one savoury dish that is made using at least four basic techniques and one sweet dish that uses three more complex techniques.

Cut out or download the recipes and, as a class activity, use the recipes to make a collage.

TASK 4

Triples: try your hand at the matching game. This is a group task.
Select ten food preparation techniques.
Make up three sets of cards:

- Mark the first set with the name of each food preparation technique.
- Mark the second set with a description of each food preparation technique.
- Mark the third set with the specific pieces of equipment you would use to carry out the techniques (you could draw a picture on these cards).
- Turn the cards over.

- Try to match the cards marked with the descriptions and pieces of equipment to the correct food preparation techniques.
- Swap your game with another group.

MAKE THE LINK

CDT – working safely with equipment to make items.

English – developing research skills and extracting the key points from information.

Art and Design – being creative to produce attractive cookery cards, the bookmark and the triples game.

Maths – developing your knowledge of shapes and sizes.

DID YOU KNOW?

Resting pastry in the refrigerator allows it to relax and this prevents the dough from shrinking when baked in a hot oven. For the best results in cake baking, let the eggs, butter and milk reach room temperature before you mix them. This makes the cake lighter.

OUR EVERYDAY LIVES

The more practice you have using a range of food preparation techniques, the more skilled you will become. The more skilled you become, the more confident you will get and you will be able to master carrying out more than one recipe at a time. All cooks learn tricks and techniques in the kitchen to help them take shortcuts.

TOP TIP
Always use the right knife for the right purpose, such as a vegetable knife or paring knife for preparing vegetables and a cook's knife for dicing them.

THE HEAT IS ON

COOKING PROCESSES

Stewing – food is cut up into small pieces and cooked in very little liquid at a low temperature for a long period of time. Both the food and the liquid are eaten, which helps to retain the nutrients. This method of cooking is good for **fruit** and cheaper cuts of meat such as **shoulder steak**.

Poaching – food is cooked in a liquid that comes halfway up the food at a temperature just below that used for simmering (usually 73°–93°C). This is used for more delicate foods such as **fish, eggs, pears, peaches**.
Steaming – food is cooked in steam only, which helps to preserve the nutrients. This is also a good method for cooking **vegetables** and delicate foods such as **fish**.

Baking – prepared foods are cooked in a pre-heated oven. Foods are usually placed on a baking tray or in a shaped container to help them keep their shape. This is used for **cakes, biscuits, potatoes** and **fruit** such as **apples**.

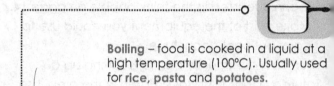

Boiling – food is cooked in a liquid at a high temperature (100°C). Usually used for **rice, pasta** and **potatoes**.
Simmering – food is cooked more gently in a liquid to prevent it breaking up or becoming tough (just below 100°C). Usually used for **bolognaise sauces, meat casseroles, soup**.

Shallow frying – food such as **steaks, sausages** and **eggs** are cooked in a pre-heated pan with a small amount of
Stir frying – a quick method of cooking whereby food such as **vegetables** and **good-quality cuts of meat** are continua stirred, usually in a wok.

Grilling – food is cooked from a direct heat source such as an electric or gas grill. Grilling is a healthy method of cooking and is a good way of removing the hidden fats in foods such as **burgers** and **sausages**.

During the cooking process, food is cooked by one or more of the following methods of heat transfer.
- **Convection** – during boiling or baking, convection currents are created around the food and heat is transferred through either a liquid or through air into the food.
- **Conduction** – heat is transferred from a solid hot surface through the food.
- **Radiation** – direct rays fall on to the food, such as grilling.

EXAMPLE

Many pieces of equipment have been developed to help people carry out the above cookery processes quicker.

Equipment	Process	Examples of foods
Microwave/combi oven	Micowaving/baking/grilling	Meat, fish, potatoes, bacon
Electric steamer	Steaming/poaching	Fish, vegetables
Healthy grilling machine	Grilling	Lean cuts of meat, sausages
Halogen oven	Baking	Meat, fish, potatoes, cakes

14

ACTIVITIES

TASK 1

- With a partner, make up a crossword using the information about cookery processes on page 14.
- Set up a swap shop and test your knowledge with a ten-minute challenge for completing each crossword. Use the timer on the computer in the classroom.

TASK 2

Working in a group, using the internet or catalogues, investigate new labour-saving equipment available for use in the kitchen. Make up a table (below) using information about five pieces of kitchen equipment you have found.

Name of equipment	Brief description or drawing of the equipment	What it is used for	Foods that can be prepared using it

TASK 3

- Draw an example of each of the 3 methods of heat transfer and give an explanation of each method.
- Use this information to come up with a design that could be printed on a tea towel or oven cloth.

TASK 4

Working on your own, find and make a simple recipe that uses convection to cook food.

TOP TIP
To prevent noodles, spaghetti and other starches from boiling over, add a little vegetable oil to the pan.

MAKE THE LINK

CDT – preparation techniques and processes in this subject will help you gain confidence in the use of equipment.

Maths – being able to calculate timings and create the crossword layout.

English – will help you make up clues for the crossword.

Science – knowing how energy in the form of heat can be used in everyday life.

DID YOU KNOW?

Chefs pound meat not just to tenderise it; they also use this technique to flatten it out and make it an even thickness so that it cooks evenly.

A roast with the bone in cooks faster than a boneless roast as the bone conducts the heat to the inside of the roast more quickly.

15

OUR EVERYDAY LIVES

The Sunday roast is a traditional British main meal. It usually consists of roasted meat such as beef, lamb, pork or chicken with roast or mashed potato, and has accompaniments such as Yorkshire pudding, stuffing, vegetables and gravy.

It's important when cooking a roast such as beef, pork, lamb or poultry, to let it sit for a little while off the heat after cooking and before carving. This allows the meat to relax, makes it more tender, easier to carve and allows time for the juices to be re-absorbed into the meat to make it more moist. It is also important to baste the meat during the cooking process to prevent it drying out.

COMBINE AND COOK

Being able to identify and understand how to use a basic range of ingredients is essential in food preparation.

INGREDIENTS

Ingredients have many properties known as '**functional properties**'. Understanding these and how they can affect the end product is essential to manufacturers during product development.
Ingredients can also be divided into two groups:

Ingredients	Functional properties
Flour	• Contains a substance called gluten, which makes baked goods such as cakes and bread rise and hold their shape. • Contains starch, which helps to thicken sauces.
Sugar	• Adds sweetness to a variety of products such as cakes, biscuits, baked beans and tomato sauce. • Helps to add colour to products such as cakes and biscuits.
Fat	• Adds flavour, moisture and colour to foods. • Gives baked products a longer shelf life.
Egg	• Adds flavour, moisture and colour to foods. • Is used to thicken or set liquids and make them more solid, for example lemon curd and egg custard. • Increases volume and gives a light texture to cakes. • Used for coating and binding ingredients.
Baking powder	• Produces a gas to make baked products rise in the oven, giving the end product a lighter texture.

1. DRY INGREDIENTS

These are ingredients in a recipe, such as flour, sugar, raising agents, salt, cocoa, spices and herbs. It is important to measure dry ingredients accurately. Use dry measuring spoons for small quantities and scales set to zero for larger quantities.

2. WET INGREDIENTS

These are ingredients in a recipe, such as water, stock, tinned tomatoes, milk, eggs, fats and vegetable oils, syrups and juices.
It is important that measuring jugs are sitting on a flat surface and are read at eye level.

EXAMPLE

Sensory analysis is the term used to describe the evaluation of food products using the senses of sight, hearing, touch, taste, and smell. We are all guilty of 'eating with our eyes first' and can be too easily influenced by other people's opinions, especially if something does not look or smell good. Manufacturers and large supermarket chains regularly use consumers to evaluate products through sensory analysis. They use the results to adapt products before putting them on sale.

TOP TIP
Accurate measurement of ingredients is essential. If you don't have measuring spoons use the cap or spoon from a medicine bottle for small amounts.

16

ACTIVITIES

TASK 1

Class activity

a. In groups, refer to the chart on the functional properties of ingredients. Use this information to investigate **one** of the ingredients below in more detail. Include the range and uses of the ingredient.
   • Flour   • Sugar   • Fat   • Egg
b. Give a five-minute presentation on your findings to the rest of the class.

TASK 2

In pairs, Google the words 'Sensory Analysis'. Select 'Sensory Analysis – Active Kids Get Cooking' and open the page.
• What is sensory analysis?
• How it is used?
• List the sensory tests commonly used.
• Choose 1 sensory test and give an example of how it can be used in the food industry.

TASK 3

Class activity – individual sponge cakes

a. Divide the class into eight groups to make the following recipe. Each group will be using different proportions of ingredients.

Group 1 (control)

Ingredients: 50g soft margarine
               50g self-raising flour
               50g caster sugar
               1 medium egg (room temperature)

Method: 1. Place all ingredients into a bowl and mix with an electric whisk for four minutes.
          2. Divide mixture evenly between nine paper cases.
          3. Bake at 180°C for 15–20 minutes until they are golden brown and spring back when touched.

Group 2 – Use 10ml baking powder.

Group 3 – Use 100g caster sugar.

Group 4 – Use an egg straight from the fridge.

Group 5 – Use 50g granulated sugar instead of caster.

Group 6 – Use 50g plain flour.

Group 7 – Use 25g block of margarine.

Group 8 – Use 50g self-raising wholemeal flour.

b. Draw a table like the one on the right including all of the eight groups.

MAKE THE LINK

Science – learning how ingredients work together.

Maths – accurate weighing and measuring.

English – presenting results and writing conclusions.

DID YOU KNOW?

Do not add dry ingredients into wet ingredients. This is because the dry ingredients are lighter and will float on the surface of the wet ingredients. When that happens, the dry ingredients that have come in contact with the wet will form a seal and prevent the rest of the ingredients from mixing properly, resulting in a lumpy mixture with pockets of dry unmixed ingredients.
Pouring wet into dry breaks up the particles, giving a smoother finish.

OUR EVERYDAY LIVES

It is important to choose the correct sugar for a recipe. Caster sugar is more expensive to buy than granulated sugar because it has been specially made into finer even-sized cube-shaped crystals. This shape allows more air to be trapped when creaming fat and sugar together during cake making.

Group number	Appearance	Taste	Texture	Comments on end results, e.g. size and shape
1 (control)				
2 (10 ml baking powder)				

c. Carry out a sensory analysis of the cakes by completing each of the headings in the chart using the following ratings:

1 – like a lot; 2 – like a little; 3 – neither like or dislike; 4 – dislike a little; 5 – dislike a lot.

d. Comment on the final results.

INTERDISCIPLINARY PROJECT

THE GENERATION GAME

Many people have very busy lifestyles and do not have a lot of time to spend in the kitchen preparing food. They do however enjoy cooking and prefer making food from scratch rather than buying ready meals. It's time to help these people out. Design a new piece of labour-saving equipment for them to use when preparing or cooking food.

Working in groups, carry out the following tasks.

TASK 1

Using the internet, make a list of new types of kitchen equipment that have been developed over the past five years and state their uses.

TASK 2

Identify a gap in the market for a new piece of equipment.

TASK 3

Brainstorm ideas for a new product that could fill this gap.

TASK 4

As a group, discuss the ideas you have come up with and select one of them to take forward.

TASK 5

Design the piece of equipment on paper or on a computer.

TASK 6

Present your equipment solution to the rest of the class.

TASK 7

Take a class vote on the most novel solution.

18

- English – you could ask your teacher to help you refine your presentation skills.
- ICT – you could use this project to help you with your research, design and presentation skills.
- CDT – could help you design the equipment.

TASK 1

Test out labour-saving equipment to see if it really does save time. Working in pairs, one person should make a given recipe using one of the following pieces of equipment and the other should make the same recipe using traditional equipment.

Modern equipment	Traditional equipment	Recipe
Food processor	Knives, grater	Coleslaw
Electric whisk	Balloon whisk, wooden spoon	Swiss roll/meringues All-in-one sponge cake
Hand blender	Potato masher, sieve	Soup

Evaluate your findings for ease of use, time, end result and ease of cleaning.

TASK 2

Make up a portfolio of large-scale equipment used in industrial food preparation. You could visit the school canteen, local food outlets or use the internet to help you with this task.

TASK 3

In groups, disassemble a convenience food product to find out the quantities and proportion of ingredients in the product.

Group 1 – Apple pie
Group 2 – Pizza
Group 3 – Sandwich
Group 4 – Spaghetti bolognese

Step 1 – Weigh the whole product including the packaging.

Step 2 – Weigh the contents and the packaging separately.
Step 3 – Disassemble the product and weigh each of the ingredients separately (i.e. apple, syrup, pastry).
Step 4 – Record the result in a table.
Step 5 – Work out the percentages of each ingredient.
Step 6 – Report back your findings to the rest of the class and discuss whether the product is value for money.

If time allows, select one of the dishes you have disassembled and make it from scratch. Discuss, as a class at the end of the lesson, which version is the best.

THE SMART COOK * THE SMART COOK

MY LEARNING CHECKLIST

Put a tick in the column to show how you think you got on
with each statement on your Learning Checklist.

Green means you got on really well with your learning in this area.
Amber means you did well with your learning.
Red means you need to do a bit of work on your learning.

	Good to go!	Getting there	Help needed
1. I can describe a range of more complex food preparation techniques.	◯	◯	◯
2. I can compare the advantages of labour-saving equipment with basic equipment through carrying out practical activities.	◯	◯	◯
3. I can match foods to suitable cookery processes.	◯	◯	◯
4. I am aware that different proportions of ingredients can affect the appearance, taste and texture of food products.	◯	◯	◯
5. I can disassemble a convenience food product and decide whether it is value for money.	◯	◯	◯

PERSONAL REVIEW

Knowing how and when to use labour-saving equipment for food preparation will
help me in my everyday life because: _____

Knowing about the proportions of ingredients in a food product is important
because: _____

**AFTER COMPLETING THIS CHAPTER DO YOU FEEL THAT YOU HAVE MORE CONFIDENCE
IN USING EQUIPMENT AND INGREDIENTS IN FOOD PREPARATION?**

I feel more **confident** because: _____

THINK-PAIR-SHARE

- On your own, think about each of the statements on the sheet and complete each box.
- With a partner, exchange answers.
- Both of you will then share your answers with other pairs or the whole class.

QUESTION OR PROMPT	WHAT I THOUGHT	WHAT MY PARTNER THOUGHT	WHAT WE WILL SHARE
How can convenience foods be made healthier when eaten as part of the family meal?			
Which cookery processes are used the most in your home?			

My name: _____

Partner's name: _____

Date: _____

THE 'G' TEAM

The biggest enemies in any food preparation area are food-poisoning bacteria (germs). Bacteria are found everywhere; in the air, on food, on you and on everything you touch. They are microscopic, which means that you cannot see them without a microscope and that's why food covered in bacteria can look and taste normal when you eat it. If you eat foods that contain **pathogenic** (harmful) bacteria, you may develop food poisoning.

Simple **personal hygiene** and **kitchen hygiene** rules can help prevent food poisoning.

THE MOST COMMON BACTERIA

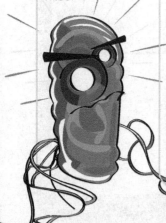

Sam

Samonella, found in: raw meat, poultry, raw eggs, unwashed fresh vegetables/herbs, pets, flies, rats and mice.

Eddy

E.coli, found in: human and animal guts. E. coli can be transferred to the meat during slaughter, and can be found in raw meat, unwashed vegetables and water. The real nasty of the G team is E. coli 0157 as it can cause potentially fatal food poisoning.

Susie

Staphylococcus aureus, found in: your nose, hair, mouth, skin, boils and cuts, prepared foods, e.g. cooked meats, poultry and foods that are handled and prepared without further cooking. This is why your own standard of personal hygiene is so important.

Lucy

Listeria, found in: soft cheeses, paté, cook-chill meals, salads and vegetables. This bacteria multiplies even in the low temperature of the fridge. It is important to check 'use-by' dates so that you do not get food poisoning.

Chloe

Campylobacter, found in: raw poultry and meat, milk and animals. This type of bacteria is the most common cause of food poisoning.

Another supporting member of the 'G' team is **Bacillus Cereus**. The easy way to remember which foods it is found in is to link the word 'Cereus' to cereals. This bacteria is found in cooked rice. Ideally you should not reheat left-over rice as this type of bacteria may not be killed. Boil rice in small quantities and serve as soon as possible. It is best to throw out any left-over rice as cooled cooked rice is a high-risk food.

EXAMPLE

The 'G' team needs the following conditions to survive and reproduce.

| temperature | food | moisture | time | oxygen | ph level |

To beat the 'G' team you need to break the links of this chain by, for example, keeping foods out of the danger zone. This means storing food at the correct temperature.

TOP TIP
Remember: 'if in doubt, throw it out'.

ACTIVITIES

TASK 1

With a partner, investigate the following:

1. The benefits of good food hygiene practices to food outlets.
2. The groups of people most at risk from food poisoning.
3. The common symptoms of food poisoning.
4. Information about two of the bacteria listed on page 22.

TASK 2

With a partner, write a reply to the following problems about hygiene on the 'Bug Busters' blog.

Dear Bug Busters

We have two pets, a dog and a cat. How can I make sure that they do not spread germs to our food?
Ida Fleas

Dear Bug Busters

I work in a hospital kitchen and have been suffering from a sore stomach and diarrhoea. What should I do?
Di Rhea

Dear Bug Busters

Why must I have my hair tied back and wear a clean apron when working in the kitchen?
Gerty Grott

Dear Bug Busters

I work in a local biscuit factory. Why do I need to wear a blue waterproof plaster over any cuts or sores on my hands?
Nieda Plaster

Dear Bug Busters

My teacher has told me I am not allowed to cook if I have long nails or wear nail varnish. Why?
Miss Vanity

Dear Bug Busters

I have got a few plates and bowls that are chipped. Can I still use them in the kitchen?
Sid Gremlin

TASK 3

Beware of the bugs that are lurking in the kitchen. Design a **Bug Buster Watch** window sticker for the kitchen.

MAKE THE LINK

Science – looking at different types of bacteria.

English – letter writing and completing observational record sheets.

DID YOU KNOW?

Not all bacteria are harmful and some can be useful in cheese and yogurt making. Swiss and Emmental cheeses are made using a type of bacteria that produces carbon dioxide gas bubbles during aging, giving them their distinctive holes. Bacteria are also essential to the production of yogurt because their role is to spoil and ferment large quantities of milk and turn it into yogurt.

23

OUR EVERYDAY LIVES

In the supermarket there are many yogurts called 'probiotic' yogurts. Probiotics, a term meaning 'for life', are living bacteria and micro-organisms that may have health benefits, such as helping the immune system stay healthy, protecting against other bacteria that could cause harm to the body, and helping digestion.

STARVE THE 'G' TEAM

Bacteria can multiply while food is transported home from the shop or during storage, preparation, cooking, cooling or serving.

CROSS-CONTAMINATION

Cross-contamination can occur during any of these stages. Cross-contamination is the transfer of bacteria from contaminated (usually raw) foods to high-risk foods, e.g. blood dripping from raw meat stored above cooked foods in a refrigerator. **You** are the **cross-contaminator** in this chain of events if you don't follow safe and hygienic practices.

The four main conditions that bacteria need to grow are:
- food
- temperature
- moisture
- time.

One way to prevent the multiplication of bacteria is to **starve** the bacteria of food and moisture. We will look at temperature and time on page 26.

FOOD

Most bacteria multiply in **high-risk** or perishable foods – they usually have a 'use-by' date. These foods are high in protein or moisture or do not require further cooking, e.g. all cooked meats and poultry, pies, mayonnaise and cooked rice. Certain foods are **low-risk** because they do not give the bacteria the nutrients and conditions they require to multiply. These foods are high in sugar, salt, fat or acid; alternatively they can be dried foods.

MOISTURE

High protein foods, e.g. chicken, meat and fish, contain moisture that allows bacteria to multiply. Dried foods, e.g. powdered milk, custard powder, gravy mix, dried vegetables, don't contain any moisture, which prevents bacteria from multiplying.

EXAMPLE

Environmental Health Officers (EHOs) handle complaints about food quality, hygiene and safety issues. They can enter any food premises at any time and inspect it for hygiene standards. They can take away food samples to be tested and make video recordings of what they see. If food premises do not implement up-to-date food safety legislation correctly they may be given time to improve any faults. If there is a risk to customers' health, then the premises may be closed immediately.

BUG WATCH POINTS – BEWARE THE STAGES WHERE BACTERIA CAN MULTIPLY!

Perishable Food	Moisture
Transport Stage	**Transport Stage**
Perishable food should be transported home as soon as possible after buying.	Food should be kept in dry cool conditions so that it does not become damp. These foods should be stored away from chilled or frozen foods.
Storage Stage	**Storage Stage**
High-risk foods, e.g. meat, should be stored in a fridge. Refrigerators should not be overloaded as this prevents cold air from circulating. Cooked meat should be stored above raw meat.	Store in a cool, dry store cupboard. Once opened these foods must be tightly resealed or placed in an airtight container.
Preparation Stage	**Preparation Stage**
High-risk foods must be prepared separately to avoid cross-contamination. People preparing the foods may transfer bacteria from raw to cooked foods via their hands or equipment.	Once liquid has been added to these foods they should be treated as high-risk to prevent bacteria breeding, e.g. stock cubes.
Cooking Stage	**Cooking Stage**
High-risk foods should be thoroughly cooked and then cooled quickly after cooking, covered and refrigerated to prevent bacteria multiplying at room temperature. They should be used within 24 hours.	These foods will now be high-risk and must be cooked thoroughly and stored appropriately.

24

ACTIVITIES

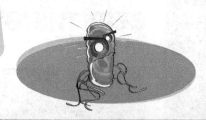

TASK 1

You are going to observe your partner on their hygienic practices in the kitchen. Discuss with your partner the points that will be observed. Use an observation record sheet (example below) to record comments while each person is making the food product.

Personal hygiene:

Kitchen hygiene:

Vegetable preparation:

Preparation of high-risk foods:

Storage throughout:

Cooking:

TASK 2

a. Working in a group of four, discuss / investigate the role of the Food Standards Agency in trying to keep our food safe to eat? Look up their website at www.food.gov.uk and select 'Scotland' from the menu on the left. Look at the sections on either Safety and Hygiene: Scotland or Nutrition: Scotland. Each member of the group should research one topic from either section. Share this information with the other members of your group.

b. Play the 'Beat the Bingo Bug' game on the same website.

TASK 3

Using available resources, investigate the role of Environmental Health in making sure our food is safe to eat.
Use your findings to produce an advice sheet for a hotel owner.

MAKE THE LINK

Science – looking at the conditions needed for bacteria to multiply.

English/ICT – research skills.

DID YOU KNOW?

Bacteria will multiply in food that has been sitting out in warm conditions, e.g. buffet foods. The maximum time recommended between cooking and serving or refrigeration and serving is 30 minutes.

OUR EVERYDAY LIVES

25

Hazard Analysis of Critical Control Points (HACCP) is the system manufacturers must implement by law to identify possible hazards during food production. Hazards such as food becoming contaminated with bacteria or objects such as glass getting into food may cause harm to people. Food manufacturers have to look at their manufacturing processes, e.g. storage, preparation or cooking of the product, and identify the points at which there is any possibility that the food they deal with may become unsafe. They then decide which controls must be put in place to reduce the risk of the hazard occuring. All food businesses, e.g. restaurants and supermarkets, must have a HACCP system in place.

TOP TIP
Use a cool box or bag to transport high-risk foods safely.

STOP THE 'G' TEAM

Another way to prevent bacteria multiplying is to **stop** the bacteria by controlling temperature and time.

TEMPERATURE

Bacteria need warmth to multiply and prefer to live at body temperature, which is 37°C.

TIME

Bacteria multiply very quickly. They will divide into two approximately every 10 minutes given the correct conditions. The size of a pinhead could contain around a million food-poisoning bacteria and after two or three hours bacteria can multiply to levels that will cause food poisoning.

BUG WATCH POINTS – BEWARE OF THE STAGES WHERE BACTERIA CAN MULTIPLY!

Temperature	Time
Purchase Stage	**Purchase Stage**
Chill cabinets and freezers have temperature controls built in for consumers to check. Freezers also have a load line and foods should be stored below this line. Buy chilled and frozen foods last when doing a large shop.	Check the 'use-by' date on the product and choose one with a long shelf life.
Transport Stage	**Transport Stage**
Do not leave chilled or frozen foods sitting in warm cars as the temperatures will rise and allow bacteria to breed. If you have a long journey, a cool bag is essential.	Take your shopping home quickly. The length of time between buying and storing in the refrigerator or freezer at home should be as short as possible.
Storage Stage	**Storage Stage**
Store chilled foods in a fridge at the correct temperature (1–4°C). Low temperatures, below 4°C, will prevent most bacteria from multiplying. The temperature of a freezer (–18°C) makes bacteria dormant or sleepy in frozen food but does not destroy them. It is advisable to defrost foods in a fridge so the temperature of the food will not rise above 4°C.	It is advisable not to eat food after its use-by date as it might be unsafe. Any high-risk left-over foods should be cooled quickly and then refrigerated. Also, joints of meat should weigh no more than 2·5kg so that they can be cooled quickly and within the recommended time of 1½–2 hours.
Preparation Stage	**Preparation Stage**
Do not leave perishable foods lying out in a warm kitchen in the danger zone, which is 5°C–63°C.	Food should be kept in the danger zone for as short a time as possible to prevent bacteria multiplying.
Cooking Stage	**Cooking Stage**
The centre of foods should be cooked to a minimum of 75°C for two minutes to destroy bacteria. Reheated foods must reach 82°C and be piping hot. Boiling water (100°C) will destroy most bacteria in 1–2 minutes.	Check that you cook or reheat foods for the correct length of time.

EXAMPLE

Two other conditions that may affect bacterial growth are:
- **Oxygen** – some bacteria require oxygen to grow (aerobic) while others can grow only in the absence of oxygen (anaerobic).
- **pH** – most food-poisoning bacteria cannot grow in acidic conditions, e.g. the pickling method of preservation protects against food-poisoning bacteria.

ACTIVITIES

TASK 1

You are going to make a chicken curry for a meal tomorrow, using frozen chicken.

Draw a 'germometer' and label it, using key temperatures and facts, to show the most important food safety facts to observe during the making of the chicken curry. This could be made into a fridge magnet.

TASK 2

You are preparing a buffet to celebrate a birthday. Three of the foods that will be served are prawn cocktail, coronation chicken and rice salad.
a. Identify the high-risk foods.
b. Explain the important hygiene controls you will carry out to make sure the food is safe to eat.

TASK 3

Read the following questions and decide on the culprit in each case. Discuss the answers with your partner if time allows.

1. **A left-over portion of chicken curry has caused food poisoning. What has caused this?**
   a. Rice has been reheated to 75°C.
   b. Curry has been reheated to 82°C.
   c. Left-over curry and rice cooled quickly.
   d. Fridge temperature of 4°C.
2. **The bacteria most commonly found in cooked rice is:**
   a. Staphylococcus aureus
   b. Listeria
   c. E. coli
   d. Bacillus cereus
3. **Which of the following foods caused an outbreak of food poisoning?**
   a. Tomatoes
   b. Egg mayonnaise
   c. Bread
   d. Gravy powder
4. **An infected cut on a kitchen worker's hand was the source of...**
   a. Salmonella
   b. Clostridium perfringens
   c. Staphylococcus aureus
   d. Bacillus cereus

MAKE THE LINK

Science – looking at how time and temperature affect bacterial growth.

Art and Design – designing a fridge magnet.

DID YOU KNOW?

'Use-by' dates may soon be a thing of the past. American scientists have discovered a natural preservative, bisin, that could extend the shelf life of some types of food e.g. fresh meat, seafood. This preservative occurs naturally in some types of harmless bacteria and prevents the growth of food-poisoning bacteria such as E coli, salmonella and listeria. The first products containing bisin are expected to be on the market within the next few years.

27

OUR EVERYDAY LIVES

The Food Hygiene Information Scheme was developed by the Food Standards Agency Scotland and applies to all outlets supplying food direct to consumers. The scheme provides 'at a glance' information about the standards of hygiene in food businesses as they are asked to display a certificate on the door or window of their premises if they have passed their hygiene inspection. The aim is to raise food hygiene standards in food outlets. You can search for information about standards of restaurants at **food.gov.uk/ratings**.

TOP TIP
Keep food in the danger zone for as short a time as possible.

INTERDISCIPLINARY PROJECT

BUST THE BUGS

Working in groups, you are going to develop a new game that can be played in one period called 'Bust the Bugs'. Bust the Bugs is linked to food hygiene practices.

TASK 1
Brainstorm what information should be included in the game.

TASK 2
Decide on the type of games you could produce with the resources available and select one to take forward.

TASK 3
Come up with a plan for making the game and then decide who will carry out each step of the plan for its production.

TASK 4
Make the game and an instruction sheet. Trial it out in your group to check that it works. Make any improvements if required.

TASK 5
Swap your game with another group and evaluate their game for the following:
- instructions for use
- ease of use
- fun factor
- length of time it takes to play
- appearance
- quality and level of information linked to food hygiene practices

TASK 6
Summing up:
- As a class, give feedback from the evaluation in task 5.
- Take a class vote on the most enjoyable game.

- English – your teacher could help with your instructions for the game.
- Maths – your teacher could help you with the sequencing of the game.
- Art and Design – your teacher could help you with the appearance and colour of your game.

28

ACTIVITIES

TASK 1

In this tricky crossword puzzle, every number corresponds to a different letter of the alphabet. Fill in the words in the crossword to try to crack the code. The letters you will not be using have been filled in. Use the letter 'E' as a starting point.

#	Letter
1	Z
2	
3	
4	
5	
6	
7	
8	
9	
10	
11	
12	J
13	
14	
15	E
16	
17	
18	Q
19	
20	
21	
22	
23	
24	
25	V
26	

19	11	7	13	10		8	11	11	20	7	24	9
6							14					
8	13	15	6	24		22	2	9	7	15	24	15
3		22					9					
15		11		10			15				17	
16			10	6	13	26	11	24	15	13	13	6
7	13	13		13		11					16	
6				3		7			3	7	26	15
	23					10					3	
	15		13	7	10	3	15	16	7	6		22
	4				5		15					
	16	7	8	15		16		22		26	15	6	3
	11					15		15				22
	10							6				6
	3	15	26	21	15	16	6	3	5	16	15	17

reheat	thaw	ill	clean	oxygen
salmonella	time	meat	listeria	rice
temperature	bacteria	defrost	EHO	moisture
boils	warmth	salt	cooking	hygiene

TASK 2

A serious outbreak of food poisoning has occured in your neighbourhood. Write an article of approximately 100 words for the local newspaper alerting people to the possible causes and symptoms of this outbreak.

29

BEAT THE 'G' TEAM ∗ BEAT THE 'G' TEAM

MY LEARNING CHECKLIST

Put a tick in the column to show how you think you got on with each
statement on your Learning Checklist.

Green means you got on really well with your learning in this area.
Amber means you did well with your learning.
Red means you need to do a bit of work on your learning.

	Good to go!	Getting there	Help needed
1. I can identify four different types of food-poisoning bacteria.	◯	◯	◯
2. I can list all the conditions bacteria need to multiply.	◯	◯	◯
3. I know how to prevent cross-contamination.	◯	◯	◯
4. I know safe practices for purchasing and storing foods.	◯	◯	◯
5. I can apply safe practices when preparing and cooking foods.	◯	◯	◯

PERSONAL REVIEW

Knowing how to transport and store food safely in my everyday life is important
because: _____

Knowing how to apply safe food hygiene practices when preparing and cooking
food for others will help me because:

_____

AFTER COMPLETING THIS CHAPTER WHAT DO YOU FEEL YOU HAVE BEEN MOST SUCCESSFUL IN LEARNING?

I think I have been **successful** in learning: _____

THINK-PAIR-SHARE

- On your own, think about each of the statements on the sheet and complete each box.
- Exchange answers with a partner.
- Share your answers with other pairs or the whole class.

QUESTION OR PROMPT	WHAT I THOUGHT	WHAT MY PARTNER THOUGHT	WHAT WE WILL SHARE
'If in doubt, throw it out.' Do you think this is a good tip? Why?			
Why do you think there is an increase in cases of food poisoning?			

My name: _____

Partner's name: _____

Date: _____

THE TREE OF NUTRITION

A healthy diet is one that is balanced. This means eating the right amount of food for how active you are and eating a range of foods to supply you with all the nutrients you need in the correct balance. The body is like a tree.

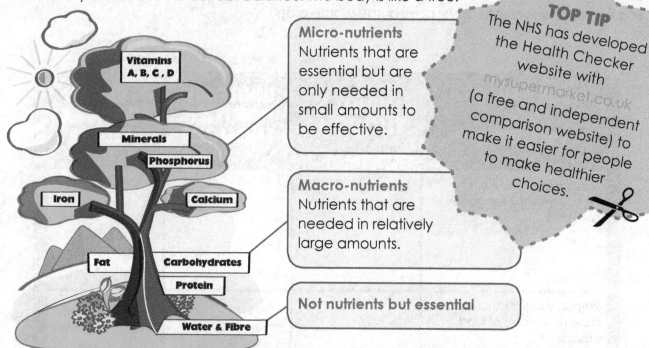

Micro-nutrients
Nutrients that are essential but are only needed in small amounts to be effective.

Macro-nutrients
Nutrients that are needed in relatively large amounts.

Not nutrients but essential

> **TOP TIP**
> The NHS has developed the Health Checker website with mysupermarket.co.uk (a free and independent comparison website) to make it easier for people to make healthier choices.

For the body to remain healthy you have to make the right choices when it comes to your diet. The following **Scottish Dietary Targets** have been put in place to help you achieve this.

Right balance: tree of nutrition will flourish

Eat more:
- fruit and vegetables,
- oily fish,
- bread (wholemeal),
- breakfast cereals,
- total complex carbohydrates.

Eat less:
- fat
- salt
- sugar

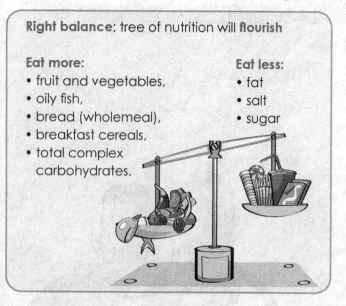

Wrong balance: tree of nutrition will wilt

Too much:
- Fat - coronary heart disease and obesity,
- sugar - tooth decay and obesity,
- salt - high blood pressure and heart disease.

Not enough:
- fibre - bowel disorders, constipation.

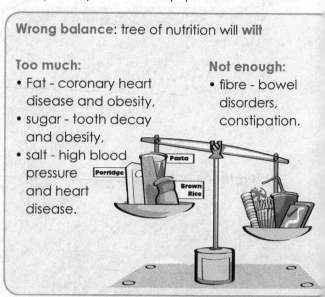

Healthy eating is essential because the wrong balance of foods will lead to diet-related health conditions.

THE WAY FORWARD

Many policies and recommendations have been put in place to advise schools, manufacturers, hospitals and care homes about how to get the balance right, such as the Healthy Living Award Scheme for the hospitality industry and the School Nutrition Policy 2008 for the provision of food in schools.

ACTIVITIES

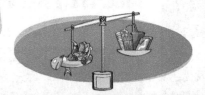

TASK 1

Part 1: As a class activity, complete the tree of nutrition by finding out the functions and sources of each of the nutrients listed.

Part 2: Use this information to make your own class wall display entitled **The Tree of Nutrition.**

TASK 2

Make your own healthy eating fortune teller.

1. Cut a piece of A4 paper into a square.
2. Fold over each corner to meet the opposite corner, then flatten.
3. Open out the paper and then fold each corner into the middle.
4. Turn over the folded square (flat side showing).
5. Fold each corner into the middle again.
6. Fold in half.
7. Mark the outside squares 1–4.
8. Open up and mark the eight inside triangular sections with the eight dietary targets, e.g. eat less fat.
9. On the underside of each of the targets make a statement of advice on how to meet the target.

Try out the game with other people in the class.

TASK 3

Draw out this Sudoko puzzle and complete it using the correct symbols.

Each horizontal row should have nine different Scottish Dietary Targets.

Each vertical row should have nine different Scottish Dietary Targets.

Each box of nine squares should have nine different targets.

Eat more bread (wholemeal)

Eat more oily fish

Eat more fruit and vegetables

Eat more breakfast cereals

Eat more complex carbohydrates

Eat less Sugar

Eat less Salt

Eat less Fat

Breastfeed

MAKE THE LINK

Maths – helps with problem solving.

CDT/Art and Design – applying the skills of designing and illustrating.

English – encouraging research skills.

DID YOU KNOW?

Fat, salt and sugar all add flavour to foods. Some yogurts claim that they are low in fat but do not mention that they can contain up to four teaspoons of sugar. We should also be careful of products that contain a flavour enhancer called monosodium glutamate (MSG), which is high in a type of salt.

OUR EVERYDAY LIVES

33

Factors that can affect our food choices are time, cost, lifestyle, foreign travel, environment issues, advertising, peer pressure and a lack of knowledge of food preparation and nutrition.

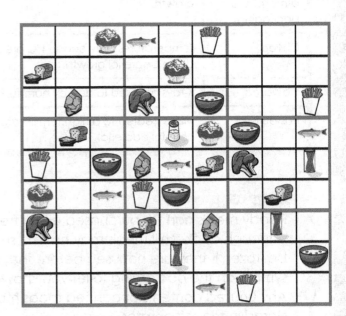

GET THE PROCESS RIGHT

Most of the foods you eat will have been processed in some way. The demand for processed foods has increased and you are able to buy a range of products that can be eaten right away instead of having to be made from scratch.

Food processing is done in two stages.
• **Primary processing:** This is the first stage. Raw produce is prepared for selling, e.g. wheat is made into flour.

• **Secondary processing:** This is the second stage.
Products that have gone through primary processing are used to make ready-to-eat produce, e.g. flour into bread.

Manufacturers have come up with a range of methods to help improve the quality and shelf life of foods. Thanks to technology, many more food preparation methods have been introduced to the food chain.

Method	Description	Examples of foods sold this way
Dried	Moisture is removed from food to stop bacteria growing.	Vegetables, fruit, herbs, spices, flour, sugar, soups
Frozen	Food is held at a temperature below -18°C to prevent bacteria growing and multiplying.	Fish, meat, chicken, vegetables, ice-cream, ready meals
Pickled/ preserved	A high concentration of acid or sugar is used. Bacteria cannot multiply in these conditions.	Vegetables, fruit, some types of fish
Salted/smoked	Smoke or salt is used to prevent bacteria growing.	Fish, bacon, cheese
Canned/ bottled	Food is sealed in cans and bottles and heat is used to destroy bacteria.	Fruit, vegetables, soups, desserts, sauces, oils
Vacuum packed	Air is removed from the package.	Bacon, cold meat, cheese, fish
MAP (modified atmosphere packaging)	Gases are changed to slow down bacterial growth.	Salad bags, vegetables, fruit
Chilled	Temperatures between 1–4°C are used to slow down bacterial growth.	Meat, fish, milk, dairy products, ready meals
Irradiated	X-rays are used to destroy harmful bacteria.	Spices, herbs, soft fruit from abroad
Pasteurised	Milk is treated to a high temperature to kill harmful bacteria.	Milk, milk products such as cheese, fruit juice, vegetable juice

EXAMPLE

Ready meals can be purchased either fresh (cook–chill), frozen, dried or canned. Although cook–chill meals may have a short-term storage life, many of them can now be frozen if they are not used before they go out of date. They will have a freezer symbol on the packaging to let you know they can be frozen.
Any unused contents of canned foods must be transferred to a plastic container and stored in the refrigerator.

ACTIVITIES

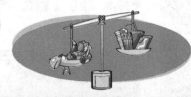

TASK 1

Group task:

Step 1: Primary and secondary processing – investigate, in more detail, what each of these terms mean.

Step 2: Select one of the following foods and map out its journey through these processes, from production (farm) to the supermarket shelf (fork).
- milk   - wheat   - beef   - potatoes

Step 3: Report your findings to the rest of the class.

TASK 2

Custard comparison

a. Taste the following types of custard: dried, tinned, chilled.

   On a comparison table, like the one below, give each custard a score from one to three using the scale below.

   The custard you like the most – 1,
   The custard you liked second – 2,
   The custard you liked the least – 3.

tard	Colour		Aroma		Taste		Texture	
	My score	Class score	My score	Class score	My score	Class score	My score	Class score
ried								
ned								
illed								

b. As a **class**, add up the total score for the class under each heading. The custard with the lowest total score is the one that is most preferred by the class.
   - Which one is the most preferred for:
     Colour?   Aroma?   Taste?   Texture?
   - Which one came out the best overall in the class? (Your challenge is how to work this out.)
   - Which one did **you** prefer overall?
     Was it the same as the one the class preferred?

c. Work out the cost of one portion of each custard. Which one is the best value for money?

MAKE THE LINK

Maths – being able to calculate the findings from the survey.

Social Studies – looking at the role of agriculture in the production of food.

English – selecting and using information.

DID YOU KNOW?

Food processing dates back to prehistoric times when basic processing incorporated slaughtering, fermenting, sun-drying, preserving with salt, and various types of cooking (such as roasting, smoking, steaming and oven baking). Salt-preservation was especially common for warriors' foods and sailors' diets.

'YARR! Why be I always so thirsty?'

SALT BEEF

35

OUR EVERYDAY LIVES

Modern food processing aims to make foods:
- edible and more pleasant to eat
- attractive
- easier to digest
- last longer
- quick and easy to prepare and cook.

TASK 3

Visit the website http://tiki.oneworld.net/food/food5.html and test your knowledge of processed foods by trying out the quizzes.

TOP TIP
Stock rotation or 'First In, First Out' (FIFO) is essential to make sure ingredients do not go out of date and are sold and consumed at their best quality.

ADDING VALUE

Nearly every method of food preparation, whether carried out in the home or in a factory, reduces the amount of nutrients in food. In particular, processes that expose foods to high levels of heat, light, and/or oxygen cause the greatest nutrient loss. Nutrients can also be 'washed out' of foods by liquids, for example boiling a potato.

Although commercial food processing helps to destroy **harmful** bacteria and extends the shelf-life of foods, the processing steps involved can result in a loss of nutrients. Some vitamins are especially sensitive to common forms of processing and storage.

Nutrient	Effect of processing
Vitamin C	Lost during storage, preparation such as chopping and/or slicing, cooking in water, drying.
Vitamin B group	Destroyed by high temperatures, exposure to light, cooking in water, drying.

Because of this, processed foods are often **enriched** or **fortified** with some of the most important nutrients (usually vitamins) that are lost during processing. There are two main types of fortification.

1 MANDATORY FORTIFICATION
This occurs when the government makes it a law for food producers to fortify particular

foods with specific nutrients, usually as a public health measure. Foods used for this purpose are foods that are consumed by almost everyone on a regular basis. Examples of foods fortified by law in this country are: margarine with Vitamins A and D and flour with Vitamin B and calcium.

2 VOLUNTARY FORTIFICATION
This occurs when food manufacturers **choose** to fortify particular foods, for example Vitamin C in blackcurrant juice, which is popular with children. Some manufacturers also use this as a way of marketing their product by claiming it is healthier.

You can fortify the foods you eat at home by adding other ingredients to them, for example adding fresh fruit such as sliced banana or strawberries to your breakfast cereal to give you more Vitamin C.

EXAMPLE
Due to the increased popularity of processed foods, manufacturers have identified a need to develop a range of foods known as **functional foods** to help people meet their dietary needs. Functional foods are those that claim to have added health benefits as well as improved nutritional properties, such as probiotic yogurts to help the digestive system and cholesterol-reducing spreads to help reduce the risk of heart disease.

TOP TIP
Remember 'fresh is best'.

ACTIVITIES

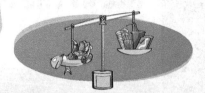

TASK 1

Visit the supermarket or look in your food cupboard at home.

Make a list of 10 foods that state on the label that they have added nutrients.

Identify the target groups the foods are aimed at and explain the reasons for the addition of the nutrients.

TASK 2

Step 1 Working individually, search the internet or magazines to find articles that make health claims about foods.

Step 2 Working as a group, discuss each of the articles you have found; then select one article the group would like to investigate further.

Step 3 Working as a group, write down in your own words what message the article is telling the public. Using the internet and other resources available to you, investigate the claim that is being made to find out if it is fact or fiction.

Step 4 Present your findings to the rest of the class.

TASK 3

A first year university computing student is concerned about eating a proper diet – she has many lectures to attend and is worried that a lack of time will make her eat more processed foods than fresh.

Design a mouse mat for this student to show practical ways of combining processed foods with fresh foods to help maintain a healthy and balanced diet.

TASK 4

Come up with a new snack for a nursery school based on the tree of nutrition (page 32). Make the snack, photograph it and evaluate its suitability for the nursery school. Suggest any changes you might want to make and come up with an exciting name for the snack.

MAKE THE LINK

English – reading and interpreting information.

Art and Design/CDT – application of design and colour.

ICT – researching information.

Science – learning about the stability of nutrients in food.

DID YOU KNOW?

Diets that lack variety can be deficient in certain nutrients. Sometimes the staple foods of a region, e.g. rice in India, can lack particular nutrients due to the soil of the region. Therefore the addition of nutrients to staple foods can prevent large-scale deficiency diseases.

In the UK, since the 1940s, there has been mandatory fortification of white flour with calcium.

OUR EVERYDAY LIVES

Organic foods are those produced without the use of chemicals and pesticides. Consumers may choose to buy organic fruit, vegetables and meat because they believe they are more nutritious than other foods. However, there is a lot of debate about whether this is true or not.

INTERDISCIPLINARY PROJECT

UP FOR DEBATE

'FRESH VERSUS PROCESSED': WHICH IS THE BEST?

Divide the class into three panels and give each of them one of the following tasks to investigate.
Panel 1 – Motion for 'Fresh is best'
Panel 2 – Motion for 'Processed is best'
Panel 3 – Judging panel. Look at both motions to help with judging

TASK 1

Panels 1 and **2** should brainstorm and write down all the points that support the motion they have been given to investigate.
Panel 3 should write down on a piece of A3 paper as many advantages and disadvantages as possible for both methods of purchasing foods (fresh and processed).

TASK 2

Panels 1 and **2** should carry out some research and start building up a presentation to put forward their motion. The presentation can take any form (PowerPoint, poster, leaflet, talk, etc.).
Panel 3 should research each motion and come up with a set of three different questions to ask each of the panels.

TASK 3

Panels 1 and **2** should nominate a speaker to put forward the motion on behalf of their panel. The rest of the panel should be prepared to answer questions from the judging panel.
Panel 3 should nominate a chairperson who will ask **panels 1** and **2** the three questions.

TASK 4

The nominated speakers on both **panel 1** and **panel 2** should put forward the motion on behalf of their panel.
The **panel 3** chairperson should put the three questions to both panels.

TASK 5

The judging panel should vote for the panel that gave the best overall performance.

• English – you could ask the teacher to help you with your debating skills.

• Drama – your teacher could help you with your voice projection.

• ICT – your teacher could help you access research sites.

ACTIVITIES

TASK

a. Divide a paper plate into the five sections of the Eatwell Plate and name each section.

b. Think about all the foods you ate yesterday and write down the number of portions of foods you ate on each section of your plate.

c. Draw out the following table and complete it using the information on your plate.

d. Work out the percentages of your diet using the information and place them into your table. How to work out percentages.

   1. Add all the portions on each section of your plate together to give you a total.

   2. For each section divide the number of the portions you have eaten by your total number of portions, then multiply this total by 100.

e. Do you think your plate is balanced? Give reasons for your answer.

f. Match the Scottish Dietary Targets to the Eatwell Plate.

g. Draw pictures of five thumbs up and three thumbs down.
Write down the five dietary targets you should be eating on the thumbs up and the three targets you need to eat less of on the thumbs down.

H. Working in small groups, cut out the thumbs and work out where they should be placed on your Eatwell Plate.

i. After a whole class discussion, glue them into place on your own paper plate.

39

	Fruit and vegetables	Bread, rice, potatoes, pasta	Milk and dairy foods	Meat, fish, eggs, beans and other non-dairy sources of protein	Foods and drinks high in fat and/or sugar
Number of portions from each section					
Recommended number of portions and % from each section	5–8 (33%)	4–5 (33%)	2–3 (15%)	2–3 (15%)	1–2 (7%)
Did you eat more or less than the recommended number of portions?					

MY LEARNING CHECKLIST

Put a tick in the column to show how you think you got on with each statement on your Learning Checklist.

Green means you got on really well with your learning in this area.
Amber means you did well with your learning.
Red means you need to do a bit of work on your learning.

Good to go! Getting there Help needed

1. I know the functions and sources of macro- and micro-nutrients.

2. I am aware of the effect of food processing on the nutritional values of foods.

3. I am now aware of how manufacturers can improve the nutritional value of food products by fortification.

4. I am able to draw a conclusion about the use and value of 'fresh versus processed foods'.

5. I can match the Scottish Dietary Targets to the sections of the Eatwell Plate.

PERSONAL REVIEW

Knowing what nutrients I should be eating in my everyday life will help me make more informed choices about food because: _____

Knowing about functional foods will help me because: _____

AFTER COMPLETING THIS CHAPTER DO YOU FEEL THAT YOU WERE AN EFFECTIVE CONTRIBUTOR TO THE DEBATE?

I think I have **contributed effectively** because: _____

THINK-PAIR-SHARE

• On your own, think about each of the statements on the sheet and complete each box.
• With a partner, exchange answers.
• Both of you will then share your answers with other pairs or the whole class.

QUESTION OR PROMPT	WHAT I THOUGHT	WHAT MY PARTNER THOUGHT	WHAT WE WILL SHARE
Functional foods – are they really necessary?			
Discuss ways to retain vitamins when preparing and cooking vegetables.			

My name: _____

Partner's name: _____

Date: _____

A NEW LIFE

All nutrients are essential to give a balanced diet. In this chapter we will look at different groups of people to see which nutrients are important to them and also other health tips that can contribute to good meal planning. Water and dietary fibre, although not nutrients, are also essential for good health.

Eating well during pregnancy is very important to allow the baby to grow and to keep the mother healthy.

IMPORTANT NUTRIENTS FOR PREGNANT WOMEN

Nutrient	Why?	How?
Protein	A **little extra** is needed to help the unborn baby to **grow**.	Foods such as chicken, fish, quorn, lean meat, which are also low in fat.
Carbohydrates	A **little extra** is needed later in the pregnancy for the baby to **grow** and **move about** and for the mother to carry the extra weight of the baby.	Wholegrain bread, baked potatoes, rice, pasta, which are also high in dietary fibre.
Iron	**No extra** iron should be needed if a healthy diet is eaten. Iron is important for the **baby's brain development** and to **build a store** for the first six months of life.	Choose lean red meats, green leafy vegetables, pulses and dried fruit.
Calcium, phosphorus and Vitamin D	The baby needs these nutrients for **bone** and **tooth development.** If the mother does not eat enough, the baby will take the calcium from the mother's bones leaving her at risk of **osteoporosis** later in life.	Milk and milk products are good sources – try choosing reduced-fat versions. Being outside will help the mother obtain Vitamin D from sunlight.
Folic acid (a Vitamin B)	This is important for the mother so she does not develop a type of **anaemia.** For the baby it ensures that the spine develops correctly, preventing **spina bifida.**	Green vegetables with meals, some fruits, e.g. oranges, grapefruits and bananas, breads, fortified breakfast cereals.
Vitamin C	This helps iron to be absorbed, preventing **anaemia** in the mother and allowing the baby's **cells and tissues to grow**. It also strengthens the **immune systems** of both.	Citrus fruits, pure fruit juices, green leafy vegetables.

ADDITIONAL HEALTH TIPS

- Pregnant women should be careful not to eat too many foods rich in Vitamin A (e.g. liver) as this may harm the baby.
- Constipation can be a problem for pregnant women so foods rich in dietary fibre should be eaten along with plenty of water.

EXAMPLE

A suitable breakfast for a pregnant woman is shown below.
Fresh orange juice – Vitamin C
Breakfast cereals with semi-skimmed milk – folic acid, protein, calcium, phosphorus
Poached egg on wholemeal toast spread with low-fat spread – protein, iron, carbohydrates, Vitamin D

ACTIVITIES

TASK 1

Before you start these activities go to www.foodafactoflife.org.uk, then 'Other' then 'General resources'. Play the question-and-answer session, bingo or the board game.

TASK 2

a. Dear Healthy Hannah

My sister is pregnant and is already overweight. She also suffers from constipation. Can you give some advice on

1. how to prevent her gaining too much weight,
2. how to prevent constipation.

With a partner, write a reply on behalf of Healthy Hannah.

b. My sister likes to cook and her favourite recipe is for pizza. Look at the recipe below.

Base
100g self-raising flour
50g margarine
75ml whole milk

Topping
100ml chopped tomatoes,
50g salami,
½ onion,
¼ pepper,
2·5ml salt,
50g cheddar cheese

Adapt the recipe to make it healthier.
If you have time, make the recipe in class.

TASK 3

During pregnancy, it is particularly important to avoid food poisoning due to the risk of harming the unborn baby. Find out which foods should be avoided during pregnancy and use this information to produce an illustrated advice sheet on **Food Safety During Pregnancy** for a doctor's surgery.

Use the following websites to help you:

www.eatwell.gov.uk
www.eatingforpregnancy.org.uk
www.nhs.uk/Pregnancy

MAKE THE LINK

Business Education – developing structure in a written reply.

ICT – using research skills, designing an advice sheet.

DID YOU KNOW?

Vitamin K is needed for blood clotting. Babies are born with very small amounts of this vitamin in their bodies. With low levels of Vitamin K, some babies can have very severe bleeding – sometimes into the brain, causing brain damage. To prevent this, all babies are given a Vitamin K injection at birth.

OUR EVERYDAY LIVES

43

Some pregnant women think that they have to 'eat for two' and so run the risk of putting on excessive amounts of weight during pregnancy. However it is essential to monitor weight gain throughout the pregnancy to reduce the risk of having a baby with a low birth weight or excessively high birth weight, both of which can lead to health problems in the baby. Babies with low birth weight have an increased risk of poor development and overweight babies can run the risk of developing various diseases in adulthood, such as heart disease, hypertension or Type 2 diabetes. The World Health Organization suggests that an average weight gain should be between 10kg and 14kg during pregnancy.

TOP TIP

Pregnant women should eat oily fish each week to provide Omega 3, which helps brain development in the unborn baby.

A HEALTHY START

Babies can be either breast-fed or bottle-fed and between the ages of four and six months they can have solid food gradually introduced into their diet. This is called **weaning**. More starchy foods, vitamins and minerals, particularly iron, are needed to help the baby grow and develop properly at this stage.

Good eating habits start from the weaning stage and must be maintained throughout nursery and primary school.

IMPORTANT NUTRIENTS FOR YOUNG CHILDREN

Nutrient	Why?	How?
Protein	Protein is needed for children to **grow**. Children are quite **active** and may fall, so protein is also needed to **repair damaged cells**.	Use chicken and minced beef as they are easy to eat. Try to encourage children to eat fish such as salmon. Pulses such as lentils can be used in a range of soups.
Carbohydrates	Children need **energy** to play.	Starchy foods such as pasta, rice, breakfast cereals and potatoes should be filling.
Iron	Needed for healthy blood to **carry oxygen** round the body to prevent children **feeling tired** and possibly becoming **anaemic**.	Red meats, eggs, breakfast cereals, pulse vegetables. Foods rich in Vitamin C should also be eaten to make sure the iron is absorbed.
Calcium, phosphorus and Vitamin D	Children's **bones** are **developing** and **growing**. Bones need to be strong as toddlers are learning to walk. **Teeth** are also **developing**.	Children should be encouraged to drink milk with their meal – full-fat milk should be given up to the age of two, after this semi-skimmed milk may be given.
Vitamin C	Vitamin C helps tissues to **grow** and **repair** if children hurt themselves. It is also important for **fighting infections**, which they may pick up when playing with other children. It is also needed for the **absorption of iron**.	Encourage healthier snacks such as fresh fruit – these will also develop healthier teeth and gums.

ADDITIONAL HEALTH TIPS

- Meals should be colourful, tasty and fun, e.g. children could design funny face salads.
- Limit the amount of sugary, fatty and salty foods.
- Avoid too many snacks between meals, especially crisps and sweets.
- Small portions should be served.

TOP TIP
Introduce foods with a variety of flavours and textures to prevent fussy eating.

✂

EXAMPLE

A suitable evening meal for a five-year-old who has just started school is shown below.
Small baked potato with tuna and salad – protein, carbohydrates, iron, calcium, Vitamin C
Glass of milk – protein, calcium

ACTIVITIES

TASK 1

As an expert on healthy eating you have been asked along to the local nursery to persuade the children to eat their five-a-day fruit and vegetables.

You must include in your presentation:
• Why fruit and vegetables are good for their health.
• Fun ways of serving fruit and vegetables.

You could also include a quiz, role play, songs, rhymes or jingles to get your message across.

TASK 2

Make up cards for a game of snap or food dominos using the healthy foods that a primary 7 class should eat. Trial your game with other members of the class first, then trial it with an S1 class in your school.

TASK 3

Working with a partner, create a calendar for a primary one class to follow during their first two weeks in school to help them stay healthy. Using a piece of A4 paper, draw out a chart like the one below to show the first two weeks. In each box write a healthy tip for **each day** – these could be linked to the Scottish Dietary Targets, nutrients or general good health advice for this age group. Some examples have been done for you.

You could illustrate your calendar or complete it using IT.

As a class, discuss each of the calendars and select the one that offers the best advice.

If time allows, ask your local primary school to trial the calendar and to give feedback.

MAKE THE LINK

Music – creation and development of songs and jingles.

ICT – designing and illustrating the snap cards.

Maths – collation and evaluation of ratings.

Art and Design – colour design for snap cards.

DID YOU KNOW?

Additives are substances that are added to food. They are commonly found in foods popular with children. All additives have an 'E' number, which shows they are legally approved. However some of them, especially food colourings, can cause changes in mood and behaviour in children, commonly known as hyperactivity.

45

OUR EVERYDAY LIVES

Young children learn by watching others and this applies to their eating habits as well. Children love colour so parents should use as many colourful fresh ingredients in each meal as possible. Fruit and vegetables are colourful foods and if well presented will encourage children to eat their five portions of fruit and vegetables each day. It's a good idea to involve toddlers and children in the preparation of food, as this will encourage them to eat the food they make and will also develop their communication skills.

Sunday	Monday	Tuesday	Wednesday	Thursday	Friday	Saturday
1. Brush your teeth after meals	2.	3. Have fruit instead of sweets as a snack	4.	5. Eat foods high in calcium	6.	7.
8.	9.	10.	11.	12.	13.	14.

KEEP ON TRACK

What you eat as a teenager and as a student will affect your health throughout **adulthood** years. Bad eating habits at this stage can lead to many diet-related conditions but following the advice below may help prevent them.

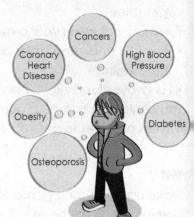

Coronary heart disease – reduce total fat intake especially saturated fat, avoid being overweight.

High blood pressure – reduce salt intake, maintain a healthy weight.

Obesity – make sure calorie intake equals energy used.

Osteoporosis – a good intake of calcium, phosphorus and Vitamin D is needed.

Cancers – antioxidant vitamins (A, C, E) and foods high in fibre are essential.

Type 2 diabetes – sugar intake must be controlled.

IMPORTANT NUTRIENTS FOR TEENAGERS AND STUDENTS

Nutrient	Why?	How?
Protein	Teenagers are still **growing rapidly** and need to **maintain** their **cells** and **tissues**. Playing sports may result in injury so protein is needed to **repair** the body.	Eat lean red meat, chicken, turkey. Pulse vegetables are important if vegetarian.
Carbohydrates	Many teenagers are **active** so need a supply of complex carbohydrates for **energy**.	Rice and pasta dishes are good starchy carbohydrates and will bulk out their diet.
Iron	The **volume of blood** increases in the body therefore all teenagers must have iron-rich foods in their diet to prevent **tiredness** and **anaemia**. Girls may need **extra iron** when they start menstruating.	Both breakfast cereals and bread are fortified with iron. Red meat should be eaten regularly and dishes such as lasagne, which contains red meat, are a cheaper option than steaks.
Calcium, phosphorus and Vitamin D	About 45% of the adult-sized skeleton forms during adolescence so it is important that bones and teeth are strong to prevent **osteoporosis** in later life.	Consuming milk-based drinks and fortified products such as bread and breakfast cereals will make sure that there are good sources of calcium in the diet.
Vitamin C	Needed for the absorption of iron to prevent **tiredness** and possible **anaemia**. Also allows tissues to **grow**, helps **cuts to heal** and builds **immunity** to infections.	Add extra vegetables into pizza toppings, spaghetti bolognese and stir fries. Use a range of colourful fruits in salads. Pure fruit juices.
Vitamin B complex	Many teenagers are **active**. Vitamin B is essential as it releases energy from carbohydrates which prevents them from **feeling tired**.	Eat wholemeal bread, breakfast cereal, green vegetables.

EXAMPLE

A suitable evening meal for a teenager is shown on the right.
Spaghetti bolognese with green vegetables – protein, carbohydrates, iron, calcium, Vitamin B complex and Vitamin C
Fresh fruit salad with fromage frais – calcium, Vitamin C
Glass of water

46

ACTIVITIES

TASK 1

Many teenagers have a sweet tooth. To help contribute to your Health Promoting school your group has decided to run a **Slash the Sugar** advertising campaign.

Include some of the following information:

- How much sugar does the average teenager eat in a year?
- What is the recommended amount of sugar a teenager should have daily?
- Why pupils should cut down on their sugar intake and simple practical ways of doing this.
- Manufactured foods that contain hidden sugars.

Your advertising campaign can include posters, leaflets, stickers, bookmarks, etc.

TASK 2

Teenagers eat a lot of fast foods – do you know how healthy they are?

Rate the following dishes in order, with 1 having **most** fat, sodium or sugar and 4 having the **least**.

Which of these has the most fat?
KFC Hot and Spicy Chicken Thighs
Starbucks chocolate-filled croissant
McDonald's Quarter Pounder
Subway Spicy Italian 6-inch sub

Which of these has the most sodium?
McDonald's Big Mac
Burger King Dutch Apple Tart
KFC Hot Wings
Subway Honey Mustard Ham 6-inch sub

Which of these has the most sugar?
Burger King fresh-baked cookies
McDonald's Hot Caramel Sundae
KFC Apple Pie Slice
Starbucks blueberry muffin

The correct answers are on page 96.

TASK 3

a. Working in pairs, develop a recipe for a teenager that is rich in both iron and Vitamin C and could be made within your class time.
b. Make the dish.
c. Calculate the iron and Vitamin C content of the dish and evaluate its suitability for a teenager.

MAKE THE LINK

Maths – calculating nutritional values, interpreting nutritional charts.

Art and Design – designing posters and leaflets for an advertising campaign.

DID YOU KNOW?

Calcium requirements are high for teenagers because their bones are growing in size and density. The amount of bone tissue in the skeleton (known as bone mass) peaks around the late twenties when bones have reached their maximum strength and density. Up to 90% of peak bone mass is acquired by age 18 in girls and age 20 in boys, which makes the teenage years a good time to build bone health.

47

OUR EVERYDAY LIVES

Research has shown that junk food can be addictive due to the sugar and fat content. In some cases, eating junk food can cause the brain to release the same chemical that plays a part in causing drug or alcohol addiction. So only have junk food occasionally as a treat.

TOP TIP
Medical advice is to maintain a healthy body mass index (BMI). Work out your BMI using the following website: www.nhibisupport.com/bmi/

HEALTH MAINTENANCE

The requirements for nutrients through **adulthood** into **old age** are similar to a teenager; however, the older you get the less active you may become and care must be taken to prevent weight gain. Also, people are more at risk of developing not only the diet-related conditions mentioned on page 46 but other conditions such as anaemia, and bowel disorders such as constipation.

IMPORTANT NUTRIENTS FOR ADULTS AND THE ELDERLY

Nutrient	Why?	How?
Protein	As people get older they tend to suffer more from ill health so protein is required for **repairing damaged cells** and **tissues**.	Foods that are easy to prepare, eat and digest such as eggs, milk, fish and chicken.
Carbohydrates	Adults need the right **energy intake** to match their **expenditure**. Too much sugary carbohydrate foods may result in **obesity** if the person is not using up all the energy supplied by these foods. The elderly in general need less energy than other age groups.	Wholegrain breakfast cereal, wholemeal bread, pulses, fruit and vegetables, which also supply vital dietary fibre.
Iron, folic acid and Vitamin C	Elderly people may be more likely to develop **anaemia** at this stage in life, therefore a diet rich in all three of these nutrients is essential as they all work together to prevent anaemia.	Foods such as red meat, liver, oily fish, bread and pulses should be eaten at meal times along with food or drink rich in Vitamin C, such as pure orange juice.
Calcium, phosphorus and Vitamin D	As people grow older **bone strength** needs to be maintained. These nutrients work together to help prevent **osteoporosis**.	Milk, cheese, oily fish and eggs should all be included in meals to supply these nutrients. Sunlight also helps.

ADDITIONAL HEALTH TIPS

- Less fat, especially saturated fat, should reduce the risk of obesity and heart disease.
- Unsaturated fats contain essential fatty acids. Omega 3 is an important fatty acid as it reduces the risk of blood clotting and so lessens the risk of heart disease and strokes.
- As people grow older and their taste buds deteriorate, their intake of salt may increase leading to a risk of high blood pressure. Reduce salt intake.

EXAMPLE

A suitable snack lunch for an elderly person is shown below.

Lentil soup – protein, iron
Ham, cheese and salad sandwich with wholemeal bread – protein, carbohydrates, calcium, Vitamin C

ACTIVITIES

TASK 1

Look at the following meals eaten by an elderly person and suggest changes to make them healthier.

Breakfast
Porridge with cream
Slice of white bread, toasted, with butter

Mid morning
Cup of tea and a cake

Lunch
Cup of tea and a cheese sandwich

Tea time
Minced beef pie, chips and peas
Cup of tea and a cake

Discuss your recommendations as a class.

TASK 2

Dear Healthy Hannah

My gran suffers from high blood pressure. Can you tell me what this is?

What can I do as a teenager so that I do not develop this condition in later life?

Write a reply to this letter.

TASK 3

Elderly people like soup and soft puddings because they are easy to eat. Many prefer home-made products, but find it difficult to prepare all of the ingredients.

a. Working in pairs, use a maximum of three store-cupboard ingredients and three fresh or frozen vegetables from those available to make a soup that is more 'home-made'.

b. Working in pairs, use tinned apples to prepare a dessert that would be easy for an elderly person to make.

TASK 4

Working in pairs, use the resources available to find out about cutting, slicing and cooking equipment that could make food preparation easier for an elderly person with arthritis.

Take one piece of equipment you have found and write down why you think it would be a good choice for this person.

MAKE THE LINK

English – letter-writing skills, research skills.

CDT – equipment design.

DID YOU KNOW?

The average life expectancy in the UK today is about 80 years, which is ten years more than it was in 1959. It is thought that by 2060 most people can expect to live a further ten years. However, for many people these extra years will be spent in ill health, which may have been caused by a poor diet. Now is the time to make changes to your diet and lifestyle so that you can have a healthier old age.

OUR EVERYDAY LIVES

49

One in eight people aged over 75 years suffers from failing eyesight. Vitamin A is an antioxidant found in some fruits and vegetables and may help to protect against poor eye health in later life – so eating foods such as kiwi fruit, grapes, spinach and broccoli regularly is a good idea.

TOP TIP
Eating little and often is easier on an elderly person's digestive system.

INTERDISCIPLINARY PROJECT

SUPER HEALTH GUIDE

TASK

Working in groups, develop a set of informative and colourful leaflets on nutritional needs and meal planning for different groups of people.

The leaflets must be suitable for distribution to your local supermarket.

Your teacher will tell you which of the following groups you will target.

- babies
- toddlers
- teenagers
- pregnant women
- the elderly

Stage 1: As a class, discuss and decide the titles and layout of the leaflets so that they are all the same.

Stage 2: Produce your leaflet using the following headings.
- The name of the group you have been given to investigate.
- The nutritional needs of the group.
- Any other helpful top tips for the group.
- A quick recipe that can be made in 30 minutes to help the group meet its needs.

Stage 3: Make up a food order sheet and a plan of work to produce the recipe.

Stage 4: Make the recipe. Take a picture of the finished dish. This can feature on your leaflet.

Stage 5: Time to evaluate your work. As a class, devise a method of evaluating the five sets of leaflets for presentation, content, ease of understanding, usefulness, etc. For example, use a tick-box sheet of questions, written comment bank or a graffiti wall.

MAKE THE LINK

- English – you could ask the teacher to help you with presentation skills.
- IT – you could practise using the interactive whiteboard.
- Art and Design – you could ask the teacher about the design and colour scheme for the leaflets.

ACTIVITIES

TASK 1

Part 1: You may be perfectly healthy at the moment but what you eat now can affect your health in later life. Some of the diet-related illnesses listed below were mentioned earlier. Investigate one of them, as a group, so you will know what may lie ahead for you if you don't pay attention to what you eat.

- heart disease
- osteoporosis
- anaemia
- bowel disorders
- obesity

Part 2: Build a lesson to teach the rest of the class about the illness or condition you have investigated. Your lesson must include the following.

- The causes of the condition.
- The effects the condition has on health.
- How to prevent the condition.

Part 3: Make your best effort as the other class members will evaluate your teaching using the criteria in the table below, giving a rating of 1 to 3 (1 = very good, 2 = satisfactory, 3 = could improve). Use a chart like the one below for the evaluation.

Criteria	Group 1	Group 2	Group 3	Group 4	Group 5
Causes given					
Effects on health given					
How to prevent it					
Whole team participation					
Interesting and enjoyable					

TASK 2

Pick one of the age groups from this chapter. Make up a wordsearch to include ten key words related to the foods the group should eat and why.

51

MY LEARNING CHECKLIST

Put a tick in the column to show how you think you got on with each statement on your Learning Checklist.

Green means you got on really well with your learning in this area.
Amber means you did well with your learning.
Red means you need to do a bit of work on your learning.

	Good to go!	Getting there	Help needed
1. I am aware of the nutrients that need to be included when planning meals for:			
• Pregnant women	○	○	○
• Babies and small children	○	○	○
• Teenagers and students	○	○	○
• Adults and the elderly	○	○	○
2. I am able to make changes to recipes and menus to make them suitable for the needs of different groups.	○	○	○
3. I am able to plan, prepare and evaluate a dish for a chosen group of people.	○	○	○

PERSONAL REVIEW

Knowing why different groups of people require particular nutrients important in my everyday life because:

_____

Knowing how to plan, prepare and cook foods suitable for specific groups is important because:

_____

AFTER COMPLETING THIS CHAPTER DO YOU FEEL YOU CAN TAKE MORE RESPONSIBILITY FOR PLANNING MEALS FOR OTHERS?

I think I can show that I am more **responsible** by: _____

THINK-PAIR-SHARE

- On your own think about each of the statements on the sheet and complete each box.
- Exchange answers with a partner.
- Both of you will then share your answers with other pairs or the whole class.

QUESTION OR PROMPT	WHAT I THOUGHT	WHAT MY PARTNER THOUGHT	WHAT WE WILL SHARE
Fast foods – are they really addictive?			
Why is it important to develop good eating habits in young children?			

My name: _____

Partner's name: _____

Date: _____

UNDER PAR

A balanced diet containing all the essential nutrients is important for everyone. However, the dietary needs of some individuals may differ and this could make it more difficult for them to achieve a balanced diet.

When someone is ill or recovering from an illness, accident or operation then it may be necessary to make some changes to their normal diet to help them recover. If the illness is serious, then the doctor may refer them to a **dietician** to advise them which foods they should eat for their condition. When the person is **convalescing** (recovering) they will need foods that will make up for the loss of nutrients and strength, e.g. loss of protein and calcium as a result of a bone fracture.

IMPORTANT NUTRIENTS FOR INVALIDS AND CONVALESCENTS

Nutrient	Why?	How?
Protein	If someone is **recovering** from an **accident** or **operation**, protein is needed to **repair** body cells and tissues.	If appetite is poor, then milk-based drinks and/or foods should be eaten. Steamed or grilled fish and chicken and eggs (e.g. omelettes) are easy to digest.
Carbohydrates	These are still required but care must be taken not to eat too many sugary foods. This can result in **weight gain** as less energy is used when recovering from illness.	Porridge is a good start to the day and will also give B vitamins, calcium, potassium and magnesium. Many starchy foods also supply dietary fibre to prevent constipation.
Iron, Folic Acid	If **blood** has been **lost** due to injury or operation, iron and folic acid will be needed to **replace** it.	Eggs, dried fruit and red meat (e.g. mince) are easy to eat.
Calcium, phosphorus and Vitamin D	If a **bone** has been **broken** or **fractured** then all three nutrients will help the bone to **heal**.	Milk, yogurt, mousses or sauce served with fish are all easy to digest.
Vitamin C	To help **iron absorption** and build up the **immune system**.	Fresh fruit juice. Eat plenty of blackcurrants, berries, citrus fruits and kiwi fruit.

ADDITIONAL HEALTH TIPS
- Water should be available to replace fluid lost through perspiration or illness.
- The total energy value of the food should be lower than normal because the recovering person will be less active.
- Avoid serving fried food, highly spiced food, rich pastries and biscuits as these may be difficult to digest.

TOP TIP
Serve colourful, appetising foods in small portions. 'Little and often' is best.

EXAMPLE
The meal below is an example of breakfast for an invalid.
Wholegrain cereal with milk – protein, calcium, iron
Boiled egg with wholemeal toast – protein, iron, carbohydrate
Fruit juice – Vitamin C

ACTIVITIES

TASK 1

Your friend is just out of hospital after having her appendix removed and she has lost her appetite. Her mother has asked your advice about which foods to give her to help her to recover and ways in which she could encourage her to eat. Develop an advice sheet for her mother.

If you have time, come up with and prepare one dish her mother could make.

TASK 2

Adapt the following meals for an elderly person who is recovering from an illness.

Breakfast
Fried egg on toasted white bread
Cup of tea

Lunch
Cream of vegetable soup
Pitta bread filled with chicken curry
Glass of water

Evening meal
Fried fish and chips
Chocolate fudge cake and cream
Diluted orange squash

TASK 3

Develop a game called 'What Food Am I?' Working in pairs, identify six foods that would be advisable for someone who is in hospital recovering from an accident to include in their diet when they get home.

Devise three clues for each food. The clues must not mention the name of the food.

Taking it in turn, each pair should read out their clues to the rest of the class and see if they can guess the food.

Once all the foods have been guessed, as a class make them into a set of cards that could be given to an occupational therapist in a hospital to play with patients.

Why not try making up the clues in another language you are studying?

MAKE THE LINK

English – creative words for describing foods.

Science – understanding the effect of nutrients on health.

Modern Languages – translating clues into a foreign language.

DID YOU KNOW?

Hospitals enhance meals for seriously ill patients by adding rich nutritional supplements to the meals they eat.

These supplements are in a powder that is added during the cooking process or as a flavoured liquid drink.

Housebound patients are often prescribed a liquid supplement to increase their nutritional intake, especially of Vitamin D.

If you are recovering from a broken bone, you should not consume certain fizzy drinks or other foods that may contain phosphoric acid. This substance allows calcium to escape from the bones, slowing down recovery.

OUR EVERYDAY LIVES

Herbal remedies have been used by cultures around the world for centuries. There are Chinese herbal medicines that have been around for approximately 3000 years, as well as Roman, Greek, Egyptian and Indian herbal remedies. Some people use these to help recovery but medical advice should always be taken before use.

ON PAR

For someone taking part in serious sporting activities such as the Olympics, eating well is important as it helps improve performance and stamina. Nutritional needs vary according to the sporting activity.

IMPORTANT NUTRIENTS FOR PEOPLE WHO PLAY SPORT

Nutrient	Why?	How?
Protein	Protein is needed to help **build muscles** and **repair** body tissues damaged by **injury**.	Poultry, white and oily fish, lean red meat dishes, eggs, cheese and milk.
Carbohydrates	Carbohydrate-rich foods help to build up **energy stores** in the muscles, which are needed during long energetic activities. Slow-release carbohydrates are better.	Complex carbohydrates such as rice, pasta, bread, potatoes, pulses and breakfast cereals should all be included in meals.
Vitamin B complex	**Some extra** Vitamin B complex may be needed by those athletes who take part in very vigorous activities. It helps to **release energy**.	Fortified breakfast cereals, bread, wholegrain cereals, green leafy vegetables, meat, eggs.
Calcium	**Joints** are subjected to **stress** and **strain** through sporting activities. Calcium is needed to ensure that a **strong skeleton** is maintained.	Milk, cheese, yogurt, flour, canned fish, green vegetables.
Iron and Vitamin C	A lack of iron can **reduce** exercise **performance**. Athletes with low iron stores often complain of tiredness and **muscle fatigue**. Vitamin C helps **iron** to be **absorbed**.	Red meat (e.g. minced meat or steak), eggs, dried fruit. Vitamin C from citrus fruits and green leafy vegetables.

ADDITIONAL HEALTH TIPS

- The more a person perspires, the more they need to drink to prevent dehydration.
- If you take part in lots of physical activity or regularly enjoy sports and exercise, you will be using up lots of energy. Eat enough food to match your activity level.
- Be careful of high-energy drinks as they can create a 'sugar rush' instead of the desired slow release of energy required. However, 'glucose' sweets are useful to use during intensive and extended sports activities, such as marathons.

TOP TIP
Athletes should not need vitamin or mineral supplements if they have a healthy balanced diet.

EXAMPLE

A suitable meal for a person engaged in an active sporting life is shown below.
Potato and leek soup with wholemeal roll – protein, iron, Vitamin B and carbohydrates
Tuna and pasta bake with vegetables – protein, calcium
Pancake filled with fruit, with low fat yogurt – calcium, carbohydrates, Vitamin C

56

ACTIVITIES

TASK 1

John is 15 and is very sporty. He is keen to have a healthy diet. John likes to take a packed lunch to school. His packed lunch should supply him with approximately 750 calories.

a. Think about the information from the chart on page 56, and select a suitable packed lunch from the list of foods below to provide John with the calories and nutrients he needs.

Wholemeal egg sandwich – 253 cals
Packet of crisps – 132 cals
Tuna-mayo baguette – 535 cals
Chocolate bar – 294 cals
Doughnut – 140 cals
Cheeseburger – 379 cals
Chicken fajita wrap – 263 cals
Apple – 53 cals
Banana – 120 cals
Orange – 59 cals
Yogurt – 98 cals
Glass of semi-skimmed milk – 96 cals
Can of cola – 139 cals
Glass of orange juice – 88 cals

132 cals   59 cals   379 cals

b. Total the number of calories your packed lunch supplies and compare this with what John should have. Are there fewer calories, or are there more?

c. With a partner, discuss and evaluate each of your choices of packed lunch in relation to John's needs.

TASK 2

Make a list of practical ways to include slow-release carbohydrates in a sports person's diet.

TASK 3

As a class task, discuss the use and value of high-energy sports drinks in the diet.

MAKE THE LINK

PE – linking dietary requirements and energy balance with sport.

Maths – calculating calorie intakes.

Science – recognising the different types of carbohydrates and how they can affect sports performance.

DID YOU KNOW?

It is best to wait for an hour after a snack or light meal before taking part in vigorous sport or exercise. If you have eaten a large meal, it is best to wait longer. This gives the body time to digest the food and to avoid feeling full or uncomfortable when taking part in the activity. This is also important to prevent stomach cramps when swimming. If you are preparing for some intense exercise, such as a sports competition, you may need to eat a small snack 30–60 minutes before the start of the competition.

57

OUR EVERYDAY LIVES

It is always important to be well-hydrated before you start a physical activity session, so you should drink water regularly throughout the day. Also try to drink plenty of fluids while you take part in exercise – this is even more important if the air or room temperature is high. Exercise makes the body warmer so it tries to cool down by sweating; this causes a loss of fluids through the skin.

LIFE WITHOUT MEAT

There are various types of vegetarians.
- Lacto-ovo vegetarians – do not eat meat, poultry or fish but will eat dairy products and eggs.
- Lacto vegetarians – do not eat meat, poultry, fish or eggs but will eat dairy products.
- Ovo vegetarians – do not eat meat, poultry, fish or dairy products but will eat eggs.
- Vegans – do not eat any animal or animal products such as dairy products or eggs.

IMPORTANT NUTRIENTS FOR VEGETARIANS

Nutrient	Why?	How?
Protein	For normal **growth**, **maintenance** and **repair** of cells.	Some animal products, e.g. milk and eggs, that are a rich source of protein may be eaten, depending on the type of vegetarianism. Other proteins include quorn, tofu, soya beans and a variety of plant proteins such as pulses, nuts and cereals.
Carbohydrates	For **energy**. Complex carbohydrate foods are filling and also provide **dietary fibre**.	Rice, egg-free pasta, dishes using pulses and nuts are good. Include plenty of carbohydrate-rich vegetables and fruit in dishes and snacks.
Iron and Vitamin C and Folic Acid	For healthy **blood production** and prevention of **anaemia**.	Dried fruit as snacks, lentils and beans in casseroles, fortified breakfast cereals, green leafy vegetables served with meals.
Calcium and phosphorus	For **development** and **maintenance** of bones and teeth.	Milk and dairy products, fortified soya products, e.g. milk (with added calcium), tofu, pulses, fortified cereals and bread, dark green leafy vegetables.
Vitamin D	To ensure **calcium** is absorbed and to maintain **strong bones** and **teeth**.	The main source of Vitamin D is the action of sunlight on skin. Other sources of Vitamin D are foods fortified with Vitamin D, such as margarine, some dairy foods and certain breakfast cereals.

58

ADDITIONAL HEALTH TIPS
- Vegetarians who consume milk, cheese and butter should be cautious of their fat intake. Reduced-fat versions of these foods are good alternatives.
- Sources of Omega 3 for vegetarians are nuts and seeds such as walnut, rapeseed and flaxseed as well as Omega-enriched eggs – all of which are good for brain development and cholesterol reduction.
- Too much dietary fibre can lead to digestive upsets such as diarrhoea, which can prevent the absorption of vital vitamins and minerals. Therefore it is essential to monitor intake.

TOP TIP
Vegans may be at risk of developing a type of anaemia due to a lack of Vitamin B12. They must seek advice on how to prevent this.

EXAMPLE
This is a suitable meal for a vegetarian.
Bean and vegetable stew with rice – protein, iron, carbohydrates, Vitamin C
Tofu and lime cheesecake – protein, calcium, Vitamin C, folic acid, phosphorus

ACTIVITIES

TASK 1

a. Visit a supermarket or supermarket website and research the range of vegetarian ready meals available.

b. Develop a vegetarian cook–chill meal suitable for adding to the range.

c. Prepare the cook–chill meal you have developed.

TASK 2

Here are the ingredients for a cottage pie.

200g minced beef
½ an onion
15ml flour
150ml beef stock
5ml herbs
500g potatoes mashed with 25g butter and 75ml milk
Seasoning

Which ingredients do you need to change to make this dish suitable for a vegetarian? Make the dish if time allows.

TASK 3

Quorn, textured vegetable protein (TVP) and tofu are good sources of alternative vegetable proteins.

Working in a group, find out how each of these foods is made, their nutritional value, and recipes you could create using these foods.

As a class, use the information you have found to produce a set of posters.

TASK 4

Go to www.foodafactoflife.org.uk. Then 'Other', 'General resources', 'Energy and nutrients'. Click on Jaz and Ben. Read the information and, with a partner, answer the questions.

MAKE THE LINK

RME – discussing how beliefs and cultures may affect food choices.

ICT – website research.

Art and Design – poster design.

DID YOU KNOW?

The word 'vegetarian' is derived from the Latin word *vegetus* meaning lively or vigorous. Vegetarianism has traditionally been linked to the people of ancient India. Even today, the Indian population make up more than 70% of the world's vegetarian population.
The first UK vegetarian cookbook was written in 1812. The oldest Vegetarian Society in the world was formed in 1847 in the UK.

59

OUR EVERYDAY LIVES

Approximately one quarter of the world's population enjoy a mostly vegetarian diet. It is estimated that a lifelong vegetarian will save the lives of approximately 760 chickens, 5 cows, 20 pigs, 29 sheep, 46 turkeys and half a ton of fish. Many people become vegetarian for health reasons; however teenagers often go through a 'phase' of being vegetarian for a number of reasons, e.g. peer pressure. Some research shows that vegetarians have low rates of obesity, coronary heart disease and high blood pressure.

NEEDS TO BE RIGHT

An increasing number of people are developing conditions that require special dietary needs. More medical knowledge has been gained about these conditions and manufacturers are now providing a range of food products to help these people with their diets.

DIABETES

During digestion food is broken down into **glucose**. Glucose is carried in the blood to all body cells to supply **energy**. A hormone called **insulin** is produced in the pancreas and is released into the blood to help **control the level of glucose** and to stop it from rising too high.

If someone has diabetes, the pancreas does not make or release enough insulin into the blood, which results in a build up of glucose in the blood and urine. The body then starts to use its fat stores for energy, which results in a loss of weight and tiredness. People at this stage may feel very thirsty and pass a lot of urine.

FOOD INTOLERANCES AND FOOD ALLERGIES

Food intolerance is the general term used when the body reacts badly to a certain food or ingredient. This term also covers foods that cause allergic reactions. Examples include lactose intolerance,

TOP TIP
Diabetics do not need to purchase special diabetic products – they can get everything they need from eating a balanced diet.

gluten intolerance and food allergies.

LACTOSE INTOLERANCE

People with lactose intolerance cannot digest the milk sugar called **lactose**. They may suffer from cramps, feel sick, have a swollen abdomen and experience diarrhoea after drinking cow's milk. An alternative diet is recommended using soya milk and lactose-free products.

GLUTEN INTOLERANCE (COELIAC)

People who are sensitive to **gluten**, the protein substance found in wheat, rye, oats and barley food products, can develop coeliac disease. This is when the lining of the intestine is damaged by gluten and this prevents nutrients from being absorbed. Children don't grow properly and adults often have anaemia, weight loss and diarrhoea. A wide range of gluten-free products is now available.

FOOD ALLERGIES

These happen when the body's immune system reacts strongly to a particular substance. Allergies to soya, peanuts, shellfish and eggs are the most common. Symptoms can include headaches, asthma, skin irritations and sickness. In severe cases, peanuts can cause anaphylactic shock. Some food colours and preservatives cause hyperactivity in children.

EXAMPLE

The Food Standards Agency estimates that around ten people a year in the UK die from severe allergic reactions to food. Sometimes small amounts of an allergen can get into a product by accident, even though food producers take great care to stop this happening. If there is a possibility that this could happen in a factory, the food label might say something such as 'may contain nuts'.

ACTIVITIES

TASK 1

Your group are members of the Food Allergy Task Force and it is your job to find out about food allergens (foods/ingredients that may cause allergic reactions when eaten).

a. Look up the website www.food.gov.uk or books/resources in the classroom and make a list of food allergens that should be identified on food labels.

b. Conduct a class survey on food allergies to find out the following:
   - Is anyone in the class or your family allergic to any foods? Compare the results to your list of food allergens.
   - Were any of the allergies different to those identified in the list?
   - Do you think any new foods should be added to the list?

TASK 2

Go to your local supermarket or use the internet. Make a list of products available for diabetics and coeliacs. Note any symbols used on packaging to let people know about their suitability. Make an information leaflet about the products available, including any symbols.

TASK 3

Try some recipes using gluten-free flour in a practical food preparation lesson. Compare the results against recipes for the same food that use ordinary flour. Here are two you could compare.

Gluten-free fairy cakes	Fairy cakes
75g gluten-free flour	75g self-raising flour
75g caster sugar	50g caster sugar
75g margarine	50g margarine
2 eggs	1 egg
2·5ml baking powder	15ml water
2·5ml vanilla essence	
15ml milk	
Oven – Gas mark 6 or 200°C	Oven – Gas mark 5 or 190°C

Method: for both versions, beat all the ingredients together until smooth and creamy. Divide between 10–12 paper cases.

Bake for 10–15 minutes until firm and golden brown.

MAKE THE LINK

ICT – use of the internet.

English – collation of information.

Maths – weighing and measuring.

DID YOU KNOW?

There are two types of diabetes.

- Type 1. This occurs when there is a severe lack of insulin and can be hereditary. It is treated with insulin injections or insulin pump and by diet.

- Type 2. This can happen at any stage in life and often occurs in overweight people. This is the most common type of diabetes and can usually be treated by diet.

Most health experts agree that the UK is facing a huge increase in the number of people with diabetes. In 2009, 2·6 million people were diagnosed with diabetes. By 2025 it is estimated that over 4 million people will have diabetes. Most of the cases will be Type 2 diabetes, because of the ageing population and an increase in obesity.

61

OUR EVERYDAY LIVES

People who are diagnosed with Coeliac disease are given prescriptions to use at pharmacies for basic gluten-free versions of foods such as bread, flour and pasta. A range of gluten-free products is now available in large supermarkets but they can be expensive to buy.

Compare your results using the following headings: colour, texture, flavour.

You will find other recipes to try at:
www.coeliac.org.uk
allrecipes.co.uk (search for gluten free recipes)
www.goodtoknow.co.uk/recipes/gluten_free

INTERDISCIPLINARY PROJECT

THE VEGETARIAN WAY

Your class has been asked by the Vegetarian Society to design a new website with a selection of suitable recipes. Working in four different groups, complete the following tasks.

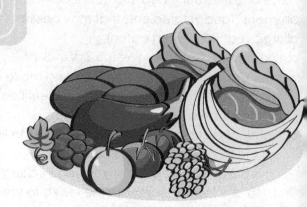

TASK 1

Each group should research suitable recipes for one type of vegetarianism.
• Lacto-ovo vegetarians
• Lacto vegetarians
• Ovo vegetarians
• Vegans

TASK 2

Investigate the range of ingredients that your group can use in recipes.

TASK 3

Develop and make one savoury and one sweet dish that would be suitable for the group you are researching.

TASK 4

Design a web page for your recipes and information about what your group can and cannot eat.

• English – you could discuss the layout and writing of recipes in an easy-to-understand format.

• ICT – you could get some help with the web page design.

• Music – you could make up a jingle or song to promote your page.

TASK 1

Working in pairs, design and make a menu card for two of the following situations.

• A family of four are visiting you for Sunday lunch. The youngest child has a peanut allergy.

• A couple are preparing a birthday treat for their four-year-old son who suffers from coeliac disease and they need help with the menu.

• It is Easter time soon and a family with a diabetic child want to throw an Easter party.

• A group of friends are getting together for a barbecue. One of the group is a lacto-ovo vegetarian.

TASK 2

In the last two chapters you have been studying different groups of people and their needs when planning meals. The list below gives some of the dietary suggestions that apply to **one or more** of the following groups:

• Toddlers
• Vegetarians
• Teenagers
• Sports people
• Pregnant women
• People with a food allergy
• Diabetics
• Convalescents
• Elderly people

With a partner, test each other to see if you can match the dietary suggestions to the people in the group. Give a reason to support each of your answers.

1. Best source of energy should be complex carbohydrates.
2. Nuts are not suitable foods.
3. May lack Vitamin B12.
4. May have to watch the intake of energy foods so that they do not gain weight.
5. Should have a good supply of folic acid in their diet.
6. Should watch the sugar content of their diet.
7. Need to have a good supply of fibre in their diet.
8. Should have adequate protein from eating eggs, dairy products and a range of pulses and vegetables.

TASK 3

Develop a snakes and ladders game.

• The ladders (up) should be foods that won't cause major allergies.

• The snakes (down) should be foods that might cause allergies, e.g. nuts.

63

MY LEARNING CHECKLIST

Put a tick in the column to show how you think you got on with each statement on your Learning Checklist.

Green means you got on really well with your learning in this area.
Amber means you did well with your learning.
Red means you need to do a bit of work on your learning.

Good to go!   Getting there   Help needed

1. **I am aware of the nutrients that need to be included when planning meals for:**
   - **Vegetarians**
   - **Sports people**
   - **Invalids and convalescents**
   - **People with special dietary needs**

2. **I know how to adapt recipes and menus to make them suitable for three different groups of people.**

PERSONAL REVIEW

Knowing why groups of people with special dietary needs require particular foods is important in my everyday life because:

_____

Knowing how to plan, prepare and cook foods suitable for groups with special dietary needs is important because:

_____

AFTER COMPLETING THIS CHAPTER DO YOU FEEL YOU CAN TAKE MORE RESPONSIBILITY FOR PLANNING MEALS FOR OTHERS?

I think I can show that I am more **responsible** by: _____

64

THINK-PAIR-SHARE

• On your own think about each of the statements on the sheet and complete each box.
• Exchange answers with a partner.
• Both of you will then share your answers with other pairs or the whole class.

QUESTION OR PROMPT	WHAT I THOUGHT	WHAT MY PARTNER THOUGHT	WHAT WE WILL SHARE
Does a healthy diet improve sports performance?			
Which of the groups of people in this chapter do you think it would be most difficult to plan meals for and why?			

My name: _____

Partner's name: _____

Date: _____

PACK IT

Nearly all the food we buy is packaged. Packaging has a number of functions.

- **Protection** – from damage, moisture loss, bacteria, insects and people touching the food.
- **Information** – ingredients, weights, storage, preparation and cooking instructions.
- **Marketing** – colour and design help persuade the customer to purchase.

The final choice of packaging material depends on the **type** of food, how it will be **stored** and whether it has to be **cooked**.

Many types of packaging are a mixture of two or more materials, e.g. a glass bottle may have a metal cap, a paper label and a plastic tamper-proof seal. Each has certain **properties**, which can have particular advantages and disadvantages.

Manufacturers are now being encouraged to make sure that all types of packaging can be recycled. The following examples show the range of materials and the products they are used for and why.

Glass **Why?** • strong/ re-usable • contents can be seen 	**Aluminium**  **Why?** • lightweight • non-breakable • easy to open (ring pull)	**Steel** **Why?** • strong/rigid • long shelf life • easy to stack in cupboard
Paper  **Why?** • lightweight • cheap to produce	**Cardboard**  **Why?** • easily shaped • easy to open • can be made in different thicknesses • lightweight	**Plastic-coated cardboard Tetra Pack**  **Why?** • keeps out air • lightweight • keeps smells and flavours in • waterproof
Plastic – rigid and flexible **Why?** • lightweight • can be moulded to the shape of the food product • can be transparent or coloured • waterproof and greaseproof • microwave, oven and freezer proof	**Modified atmosphere packaging (MAP)** **Why?** • product is packed with a gas, e.g. nitrogen, which replaces oxygen to make the product last longer and remain looking fresh	**Vacuum packaging** **Why?** • air is removed from the pack under a vacuum then the food is thoroughly sealed. The strong plastic clings to the food so there is no air present, making the food last longer

EXAMPLE

Take-away packaging should keep food hot, not allow the food to leak, protect the food as it is carried home, stand up to the temperature of the food without becoming soggy or melting and be easy to dispose of.

ACTIVITIES

TASK 1

Working in small groups, look at the range of packaging materials listed on the opposite page and identify any concerns with using them either for the consumer or the manufacturer. Report your findings to the class.

TASK 2

Role play: 'What makes **you** the best type of packaging?' Working in pairs, one of you will act out the role of being the take-away pizza box and the other will be the take-away Chinese chow mein.

TASK 3

Name three different types of food products that you think use too much packaging. Explain why, and how you think the packaging could be reduced without affecting the product.

TASK 4

An orange drink can be packaged using different materials.

a. List the types of packaging materials that could be used.

b. Explain the advantages and disadvantages of each material.

TOP TIP
Your role in recycling is to choose biodegradable packaging.

MAKE THE LINK

Drama – role play.

Science – properties of packaging materials.

DID YOU KNOW?

Tamper-proof packaging helps to keep products safe. Shrink-wrapped jars and plastic collars on bottles and jars show whether the product has been opened and the contents have been damaged or altered in any way.

OUR EVERYDAY LIVES

Containers designed to be placed in the oven used to be made of aluminium. Heat-resistant plastics are now more commonly used. The plastic does not soften when heated and, as well as being ovenproof, it can be heated in the microwave. Sheet plastic is vacuum-formed to create a shaped tray with two or three sections to contain a whole meal.

Ovenproof paperboard is also designed for use in a microwave. Paperboard is coated with heat-resistant plastic and formed into trays. This allows the tray to withstand temperatures from -40°C to 230°C, so the product can be stored in the freezer and then the tray can withstand cooking in an oven or microwave.

67

WHAT MUST A FOOD LABEL TELL YOU?

Information is provided on the packaging of food products to help consumers choose between different foods, brands and flavours. Much of the information that is provided on the label has to be there by law – this is called **statutory labelling**. As part of the EU, the UK has to conform to the law.

THE EIGHT STATUTORY PIECES OF INFORMATION ON A LABEL

Preparation and/or **cooking** instructions to make sure the food is safe to eat.

The **name of the food** or a **description** if the name alone does not clearly describe the food.

Weight or **volume** using the 'e' symbol to show average weight.

Shelf life to make sure the food is safe to eat and at it's best quality.

Storage instructions to ensure the quality and safety of food.

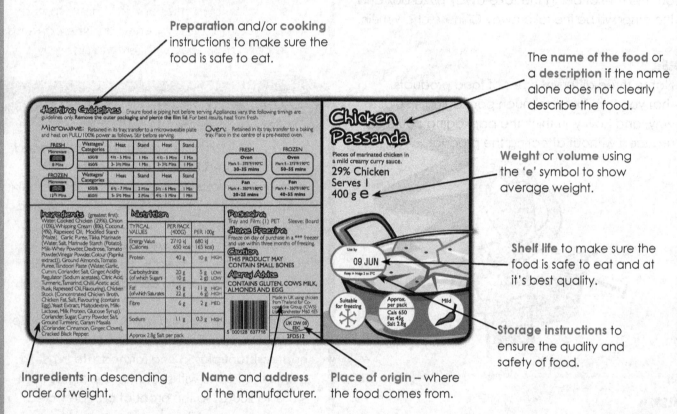

Ingredients in descending order of weight.

Name and **address** of the manufacturer.

Place of origin – where the food comes from.

EXAMPLE

Rules for **Genetically Modified** (GM) food labelling came into force within the EU in 2004. The presence of genetically modified ingredients in foods must be indicated on the label. Consumers are unsure of the safety of genetically modified foods and many do not realise that they are eating products containing ingredients that have been genetically modified.

TOP TIP
Labels on the supermarket shelf give a price per 100g or 100ml. Use this to get the best value for money.

68

ACTIVITIES

TASK 1

Visit the Interactive Food Label at www.food.gov.uk to reinforce your knowledge of food labelling.

TASK 2

Read the two labels for carrot and coriander soup below, both of which were purchased on 24 July 2012, and serve two people.

Answer the following questions.
1. What does the 'e' mean on the label of soup A?
2. Looking at the ingredients, which soup per serving contains the most fresh vegetables, the most saturated fat and the most salt. How do you know this?
3. Which soup could have 'contains all natural ingredients' on the label?
4. Soup A gives advice about freezing. What would be the advantage of this?
5. Soup B states that leftover soup should be put into a non-metallic container, covered and refrigerated. Why?
6. Which soup would you buy as an emergency standby and why?

MAKE THE LINK

English – interpreting information.

ICT – using websites to reinforce knowledge.

DID YOU KNOW?

The labelling rules for pre-packed foods do not apply to foods sold loose. For example, the listing of ingredients, date and storage conditions are not available unless you ask for them. This applies to foods from the bakery, butchery and deli counters.

OUR EVERYDAY LIVES

Many food products now have the ingredients listed in different languages. This is useful for people who travel abroad and suffer from food intolerances or allergies.

Information	Soup A	Soup B
The name of the food or description	Carrot and coriander soup Fresh soup	Carrot and coriander soup Tinned soup
Weight or volume	600g e	400g
Ingredients	Ingredients: carrots (42%), water, onions (7%), cream, wheat flour, butter, salt, coriander leaf, garlic, ground coriander, nutmeg	Ingredients: water, carrots (31%), onions (7%), modified maize starch, double cream (milk), carrot juice from concentrate, coriander, sugar, salt, vegetable bouillon (salt, yeast extract, sugar, leek powder, onion powder, garlic powder, natural flavouring), lemon juice from concentrate, orange juice from concentrate, ground nutmeg, garlic, spirit vinegar, coriander oil
Storage instructions	Keep refrigerated Once opened use within 24 hours Suitable for home freezing	Unopened, store in a cool dry place. Opened, pour contents into a non-metallic container, cover and refrigerate. Consume within two days.
Shelf life	Use by 04.08.2012	Best before June 2013

WISE UP TO THE LABEL

Nutritional labelling is only needed by law when a nutrition or health claim is made. Nutritional claims are statements that suggest a food has a particular beneficial effect on health or that it is 'low in fat', 'high in fibre' or has 'no added sugar/salt'. However, most food labels show nutritional information to help us make healthier choices about food products. The nutritional information on labels must be given per 100g or 100ml. Most manufacturers give the nutritional information per portion, which allows consumers to compare products.

The label can also show the amounts of monounsaturated and polyunsaturated fats, cholesterol, starch and some vitamins and minerals if they are present in large enough amounts.

Trading Standards officers are responsible for checking that all food products are accurately labelled.
Visit www.tradingstandards.gov.uk/advice/index.cfm for more details of the full range of services they offer consumers.

GROUP 1 AND GROUP 2

There are two formats – known as **group 1** and **group 2** – used by manufacturers to present nutritional information on a label.

- **Group 1** – energy in kilojoules (kJ) and kilocalories (kcal), protein, carbohydrate and fat in grams (g).
- **Group 2** – energy in kilojoules (kJ) and kilocalories (kcal), protein, carbohydrate, sugars, fat, saturates, fibre and sodium in grams (g).

GROUP A LABEL

Typical Nutritional Values	
Energy	635 kJ
	152 kcal
Protein	2.5g
Carbohydrate	17.1g
Fat	8.1g

GROUP B LABEL

Typical Nutritional Values	
Energy	635 kJ
	152 kcal
Protein	2.5g
Carbohydrate	17.1g
Fat	8.1g
of which saturates	0.9g
Fibre	0.9g
Sodium	0.22g

EXAMPLE

Fat, sugar and salt give flavour to food. To claim that a product is 'reduced fat', the amount of fat must be at least 30% lower than standard products. But these types of foods tend to be high in fat in the first place, so the 'reduced fat' version can still have quite high amounts of fat. Foods labelled 'low fat' or 'reduced fat' aren't necessarily low in energy. The fat is often replaced by other ingredients, so the product can have the same or an even higher energy (calorie) content. Also, if you're tempted to use more of a reduced-fat product than you would of the full-fat version, you might end up consuming the same, or even more, fat and calories so the product may not be the healthy choice you think it is. Many manufacturers are making nutritional claims to help promote their products but it is essential to read the label carefully.

TOP TIP
Manufacturers use Traffic Light symbols or Guideline Daily Amounts (GDAs) to try and help consumers make healthy food choices.

ACTIVITIES

TASK 1

Some manufacturers use Traffic Light symbols or Guideline Daily Amounts (GDAs) to try to help consumers make healthy food choices.

In small groups, find an example of a label that shows each of these methods of nutritional labelling.

a. Fold a piece of A3 paper in half and name one half 'Traffic Light symbols' and the remaining half 'Guideline Daily Amounts'.

b. Glue each of the labels under the correct heading.

c. Compare each type of label and decide on the one that is:
   • the easiest to understand
   • the most informative
   • the one that helps the consumer make a healthier choice.

d. As a class, discuss your findings and decide on the best method of nutritional labelling.

TASK 2

In a group, using three different types of breakfast cereals, weigh out a portion size of each according to the packet.

a. Compare the quantity of each portion size. Which one looks like the biggest portion in the bowl?

b. Look at the nutritional information on the labels of the breakfast cereals.
   Compare the nutritional content of each portion size with regard to the amount of calories, sugar, salt, fibre, iron, calcium and folic acid.
   Draw a chart to record your findings.
   Evaluate which one would be best for someone who is:
   • Suffering from heart disease
   • Trying to lose weight
   • Anaemic
   • Pregnant.

c. Overall, which of the three breakfast cereals is the best for health?

MAKE THE LINK

Maths – calculating nutritional content per portion.

English – interpreting information and drawing conclusions.

DID YOU KNOW?

Processed foods provide 75% of the salt in our diet. Just 10%–15% comes from the salt we add when we're cooking or eating. On average we eat about 8·6g of salt a day. We should try to cut this down to no more than 6g of salt a day for adults. Look at the Food Standards website **www.food.gov.uk** to see the progress being made by the Salt Campaign.

OUR EVERYDAY LIVES

Supermarkets now offer three levels of products: a value range, their own-labelled brand and a range of other named brands from independent manufacturers. It is advisable to study the labels of each carefully as the value ranges are sometimes more nutritional than the others and as a result offer better value for money.

'ADDED LITTLE EXTRAS'

Manufacturers often provide extra labelling information on packets, which is not required by law. This is known as 'voluntary' labelling and is often used by them to promote the benefits of their products.

RECYCLING

Increasing awareness of the problems facing the environment has encouraged more consumers to show more interest in conserving resources when purchasing and disposing of food packaging. A variety of recycling/disposable symbols are found on food packaging and may influence consumers' choice of foods.

Glass
The product can be taken to a bottle bank.
Glass can be used again to make 'new' glass, which is cheaper to produce.

Aluminium
Recycling is cheaper than starting from new and helps to conserve energy.

A symbol found on paper, card or packaging materials. This indicates that the packaging can be recycled.

Tidyman Symbol
Used to encourage people to recycle and put food and packets in bins, e.g. snack foods, crisp packets and cans of drink.

Plastics
The different types of plastic are identified below the triangle and each has a different number in the triangle.

VEGETARIAN SYMBOLS

The Vegetarian Society's labelling scheme makes it is easy for consumers to select vegetarian food which suits their needs.
Many supermarkets have their own logo stating that foods are suitable for vegetarians. However since many of these products contain egg or milk, they will not be suitable for all types of vegetarians.

THE ORGANIC SYMBOL

By identifying the Soil Association logo on food packaging, consumers are able to select foods that have been grown without artificial fertilisers, which may be good for consumers who are concerned about the environment.

TOP TIP
Shopping online prevents you from making informed food choices as you can't read the labels on the products you are purchasing.

EXAMPLE
Allergy information
As well as appearing in the ingredients list, sometimes foods that are known to cause allergies may be highlighted on packaging, e.g. 'this product contains milk', for those people who are lactose intolerant. Many products now have 'may contain nuts' or 'produced in a factory where nuts are also used' warnings to protect them from legal action if someone with a nut allergy eats their product and suffers as a result.

ACTIVITIES

TASK 1

Working in a group of four, come up with a poster to persuade pupils in your school to become more aware of the environment and so contribute to an Eco School award. The theme of the poster is **the Three Rs – reduce, reuse and recycle.**

TASK 2

As a class, debate the following:

- Voluntary labelling information – should any of it be statutory?
- Shopping online – what are the problems linked to food labelling?

TASK 3

Design a new set of symbols for use on product labelling to promote each of the eight dietary targets. This task can be done in groups where the labels are collated into a set.

TASK 4

Look at a range of food packaging and find a voluntary food symbol that hasn't been discussed in this book.

Draw the symbol and explain its use.

MAKE THE LINK

Art and Design/ICT – designing symbols/poster.

English – debating the pros and cons of voluntary labelling.

DID YOU KNOW?

Recycling is an excellent way of saving energy and conserving the environment.

- One recycled tin can saves enough energy to power a television for three hours.
- One recycled glass bottle saves enough energy to power a computer for 25 minutes.
- One recycled plastic bottle saves enough energy to power a 60-watt light bulb for three hours.
- 70% less energy is required to recycle paper compared with making it from raw materials.

73

OUR EVERYDAY LIVES

Due to busy lifestyles, many consumers use ready-made frozen foods that can be microwaved straight from the freezer.

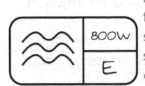

Microwave ovens and food packs display special labels to make sure that people using different ovens cook food thoroughly to reduce the risk of food poisoning.

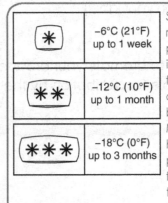

✳	−6°C (21°F) up to 1 week
✳✳	−12°C (10°F) up to 1 month
✳✳✳	−18°C (0°F) up to 3 months

Star ratings for refrigerators and freezers provide information that indicates how long the food is likely to be kept at its best if stored at below a set temperature. Many supermarkets have a symbol on the packaging of cook – chill foods that indicates if the food is suitable for freezing at home.

INTERDISCIPLINARY PROJECT

THE WHOLE PACKAGE

Your group has been asked to develop a product to add to a range of cook – chill international dishes in a supermarket. Your teacher will give each group a different country, e.g. China, Spain, India, Thailand, Italy. The **specification** for the dish you develop has to be correctly and clearly labelled with statutory and voluntary information.

TASK 1

Carry out some research into:
• the range of dishes currently available.
• the ingredients that are used.
• the cooking/reheating methods used.
• the types of packaging used.

TASK 2

Come up with a recipe for your product. Carry out a nutritional analysis of the recipe so you know what to put on the label. This can be done either using computer software or nutritional tables.

TASK 3

Make a list of the statutory labelling information that you must have on your outer packaging.

Decide which two pieces of voluntary information you are going to use.

Plan the layout of your information.

TASK 4

Make up the label for your product. You may wish to use a computer to do this.

TASK 5

Make your product. If possible, photograph your product (this could be used on your label).

TASK 6

Make up a flyer to promote your product. (NB: This flyer should be suitable for distribution by the postal worker as a postal drop.)

TOP TIP
Use packaging from an existing product to help with your planning. Decide on a snappy name for your product!

74

MAKE THE LINK

- Art and Design – your teacher may give you advice about how to make your label colourful.
- Geography – your teacher may give you information about different cultures and the food they eat.
- ICT/CDT – you could design your label.

ACTIVITIES

TASK 1

Draw a funny informative cartoon strip about the lifecycle of one of the following:
- A glass bottle
- A plastic bag
- An aluminium drinks can
- A pizza box.

TASK 2

In pairs, collect weekly class statistics on the following:
- The number and type of milk containers purchased by families.
- The number of plastic shopping bags used.
- The amount of recycling carried out.

In small groups, carry out a class survey to find out how responsible people in your class and their families are being in the recycling of food packaging and waste.

Consider other ways to reduce packaging waste.

TASK 3

When you buy foods they are usually packaged. However, you may need to re-package certain items once they have been opened to prevent them from drying out and to protect them from bacterial contamination.

Match the following foods with a suitable packaging material.

Foods	Packaging
Soup for the freezer	
Raw meat	
Fatless sponge cake	

Give a reason for each of your answers.

TASK 4

Visit the local supermarket and make a list of any packaging that is aimed at specific groups, e.g. children.

75

MY LEARNING CHECKLIST

Put a tick in the column to show how you think you got on
with each statement on your Learning Checklist.

Green means you got on really well with your learning in this area.
Amber means you did well with your learning.
Red means you need to do a bit of work on your learning.

	Good to go!	Getting there	Help needed
1. **I can list types of food packaging.**	◯	◯	◯
2. **I know the reasons why they are used.**	◯	◯	◯
3. **I know the labelling information that has to be on food products by law.**	◯	◯	◯
4. **I am able to evaluate nutritional information on food labels.**	◯	◯	◯
5. **I know the voluntary labelling information that may be on food products.**	◯	◯	◯

PERSONAL REVIEW

Knowing about statutory food labelling information is important because:

_____

Knowing how to use labelling information to improve my own and other's food
choices is important because: _____

AFTER COMPLETING THIS CHAPTER DO YOU FEEL YOU CAN USE FOOD LABELLING
INFORMATION SUCCESSFULLY?

I think I can **successfully** use the labelling information to help me make more
informed food choices because: _____

THINK-PAIR-SHARE

- On your own, think about each of the statements on the sheet and complete each box.
- Exchange answers with a partner.
- Both of you will then share your answers with other pairs or the whole class.

QUESTION OR PROMPT	WHAT I THOUGHT	WHAT MY PARTNER THOUGHT	WHAT WE WILL SHARE
Why should packaging be environmentally friendly?			
Nutritional labelling should be made easy to understand. Why?			

My name: _____

Partner's name: _____

Date: _____

FABRIC KNOW HOW

Fabrics all have **properties** linked to what the fabric is made of (**fibre content**), the way the fabric is made up (**construction**) and/or any manufacturing processes that have been applied during production (**fabric finishes**, e.g. water proofing). It is essential to know what fabric properties you are looking for when designing textile items, as it is important to select the correct fabrics for the design to be successful.

PROPERTIES

Absorbency, crease resistance, durability (hard wearing), ease of care, elasticity, flammability, insulation, resistance to mildew, stain resistance, strength, warmth, colourfast, shrink resistant, waterproof, windproof

FIBRE CONTENT

Natural – cotton, wool, linen, silk
Synthetic – polyester, nylon

CONSTRUCTION

Woven, knitted, bonded

If you decide to purchase a textile item rather than make it yourself it is still important to know what it is made from so it can be looked after properly. The fibre content in clothing and textile items has to be on the label in the UK.

The inclusion of washing instructions is not mandatory in the UK. However it is strongly advised and a set of symbols has been developed for use throughout Europe. The main Care Labelling Symbols are shown here.

Symbols	Description	Meaning
Wash tub	Wash tub	The washing process by machine or hand
Triangle	Triangle	Chlorine bleaching
Iron	Iron	Ironing
Circle	Circle	Dry cleaning
Circle in square	Circle in square	Tumble drying (after washing)
Cross	Cross	Do not

EXAMPLE

More than one fibre can be combined to improve the overall properties of a fabric, for example polyester is easier to care for as it doesn't crease and cotton is more comfortable to wear but hard to iron. By combining them both to make polyester cotton it becomes an easy-to-care-for fabric that can be used for everyday items such as shirts, blouses and bed linen.

TOP TIP
Always check the care label on everyday clothing such as school uniform to make sure it does not have to be dry cleaned as this makes it more difficult and costly to look after.

78

ACTIVITIES

TASK 1

You have been asked to design a new sports kit for the PE department in your school.

Working with a partner, complete the following.

a. Copy out the following table. Give two fabric properties required for each item of clothing.

b. Explain the importance of the fabric properties you have chosen for each item of clothing.

Items in a sports kit	Fabric properties required	Why are the fabric properties important?
T-shirt	1. Crease-resistant 2.	1. The t-shirt has to look good and will be transported to school in a bag.
Shorts		
Jogging bottoms		
Socks		
Swimwear		

TASK 2

Fabric is used to make many items **other than clothing**. Working in three groups, your teacher will give you one of the following categories to brainstorm:

• Household items

• Types of transport

• Outdoor activities.

a. Write the name of your category on a piece of poster paper. This is your 'graffiti wall'. You will be given ten minutes to write down all the items that use any type of fabric in this category.

b. Move to the next group's 'wall' and add any other items to the poster paper. You will be given five minutes for this.

c. Move to the last wall and again add any other items you can think of.

d. Move back to your own wall and report back the findings to the rest of the class.

As a class use the information you have found to make a wall display for the classroom.

MAKE THE LINK

Maths – working within time constraints.

English – reading a label and interpreting information.

PE – understanding the fabric properties of items in a sports kit.

DID YOU KNOW?

Bamboo fabric is cloth made from natural bamboo fibres. It is lightweight with a soft texture, similar to cashmere, and feels luxurious against the skin. Best of all, bamboo is a fast-growing plant, making it an environmentally friendly choice. It is more absorbent than cotton and has natural anti-bacterial properties so it helps prevent body odours on the fabric. Wrinkles fall out quickly and there is no annoying static cling, making it an ideal fabric for many items of clothing.

79

OUR EVERYDAY LIVES

The reaction of textiles to fire (in other words, what happens to them when they are exposed to fire or a heat source) is governed by International, European and British legislation. This means that there are laws written to protect consumers. Nightwear, bed linen, curtains in hotels and public buildings, protective clothing, furniture and upholstery fabrics should all meet agreed flammability standards.

TASK 3

Look up the website www.care-labelling.co.uk about care labelling. Design and make up a laminated card to stick on a pinboard to explain the meaning of all the care labelling symbols.

FABRIC IN ACTION

Textile items are made by joining different pieces of fabrics together either by machine or by hand. The shapes of the fabric pieces need to be accurately worked out before you start cutting out the fabric. Each shape must be drawn on paper to produce a pattern. You can either buy a ready-made pattern from a fabric shop or make up your own pattern.

LET'S GET STARTED!

Decide on the paper pattern you are going to use. Once you have done this, choose the fabric you want to use. Remember to consider the properties of the fabric when doing this.

The next stage is to follow a series of basic steps to make it up.

More complicated items will require the use of more difficult machine and/or hand-sewing skills. They may also involve the use of items such as buttons and zips (notions) or involve more intricate designs such as the use of appliqué and embroidery.

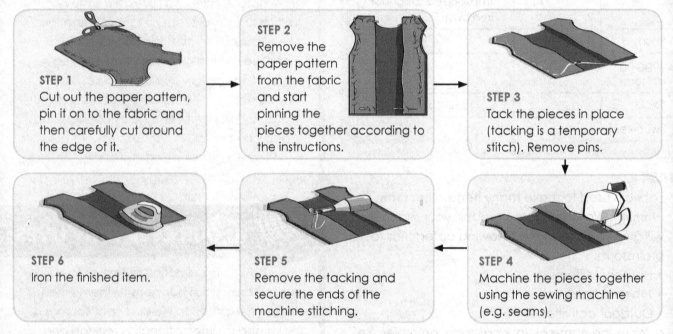

STEP 1
Cut out the paper pattern, pin it on to the fabric and then carefully cut around the edge of it.

STEP 2
Remove the paper pattern from the fabric and start pinning the pieces together according to the instructions.

STEP 3
Tack the pieces in place (tacking is a temporary stitch). Remove pins.

STEP 6
Iron the finished item.

STEP 5
Remove the tacking and secure the ends of the machine stitching.

STEP 4
Machine the pieces together using the sewing machine (e.g. seams).

Colour is also important when designing a textile item. It can set a mood, attract attention, or make a statement. By selecting the right colour scheme, you can create a feeling of elegance, warmth and calmness, or you can convey liveliness and cheerfulness. Colour can be the most powerful design element if you learn to use it effectively. Colour affects us in numerous ways, both mentally and physically. Strong red has been shown to raise blood pressure, while blue has a calming effect.

Colour can be added in a variety of ways. The use of dyes, paints, embroidery, appliqué, buttons and zips are a few examples of how to add colour to an item. This is an ideal way to personalise or make your item unique.

EXAMPLE

Appliqué is when additional fabrics are attached to the main background fabric either by machine, hand sewing, or fabric glue. It is a good way to add colour and texture to a finished item. The best results are gained when the appliqué shapes are not too small as these can be difficult to attach neatly. Any small detailed design may be better applied by embroidery stitches, which can also add colour and texture.

ACTIVITIES

TASK 1

Group 1 – Investigate basic sewing equipment and their uses.

Group 2 – Investigate what 'sewing notions' are and their uses.

Group 3 – Investigate the range and cost of sewing machines available and their uses. Report your findings back to the rest of the class.

TASK 2

Make up a poster of safety rules to follow when using a range of sewing equipment.

TASK 3

Design and make a keyring from felt fabric. Your article must show all of the following processes: machine stitching, hand stitching, sewing on a button and appliqué. Use the resources available to help you do this.

Take two squares of felt (10cm x 10cm).

1. Place the two square pieces of felt together. Pin a paper circle pattern (8cm in diameter) on top. Make sure you pin through both thicknesses of the fabric. Cut around the edge of the paper pattern to give you two circles of felt and then remove the paper pattern.
2. Now make a badge for the front of your keyring. Cut out a 4-cm square of felt in any colour. Select a button and sew it onto the centre of the square of felt.
3. Now appliqué this badge by hand onto the front of **one** of your circles of felt. Make sure you choose a stitch you can manage.
   1. Now tack the two circles of felt together and insert a looped piece of ribbon with a metal ring. Follow the instructions and diagram on page 80.
   2. Now you are going to machine your two circles together. Starting with a small reverse stitch, sew 0·5 cm in from the edge of the fabric. Finish with a small reverse stitch. Remove from the machine and remove the tacking stitches.

MAKE THE LINK

CDT – working safely with tools and equipment.

Maths – practical application of measuring skills.

Science – understanding the properties of fabrics.

DID YOU KNOW?

Computer aided design (CAD) is now well established and allows manufacturers to design new fabrics. It also shows in advance how the final design will look.

Computer aided manufacture (CAM) ensures consistent results in the production of textile items. This reduces production time and the waste of materials, which in turn saves money.

81

OUR EVERYDAY LIVES

Currently the fashion industry relies mostly on mass-market sales. The mass market caters for a wide range of customers, producing ready-to-wear clothes in large quantities and standard sizes. Inexpensive materials with creative designs help to give people affordable fashion. Mass-market designers generally copy or adapt the trends set by famous names in fashion.

TOP TIP

Paper patterns have detailed instructions and come with special symbols to help you match up each of the fabric pieces accurately. There are many websites that will help you understand these symbols.

INTERDISCIPLINARY PROJECT

SETTING THE SCENE

A local hotel is opening a new 'Healthy Eating' bistro. They want you to come up with a design for a new fabric tablemat that they can use in the restaurant. The tablemat must promote their message of healthy eating.

TASK 1

Copy and complete the following table by placing a tick in the column under the heading linked to your level for each of the skills.

Skills	Excellent	Good	Satisfactory	Not very good	Very poor
Hand sewing					
Machine sewing					
Artistic talent					

TASK 2

What fabric properties would be important for this tablemat?

TASK 3

You will be given one A3 piece of polyester cotton fabric and some wadding for the middle of your mat. You must show an example of all of the following skills in your tablemat:
• hand sewing   • machine sewing   • appliqué.

Draw four possible designs for your mat (remember to consider the resources available).
Decide which design you want to do and draw up a pattern (to scale) of your design.

TASK 4

Make up your tablemat.

TASK 5

Rate your tablemat by drawing a line on the scale next to each of the headings.

Hand sewing	1 ←————————————————→ 5
	Excellent Poor
Machine sewing	1 ←————————————————→ 5
	Excellent Poor
Artistic talent	1 ←————————————————→ 5
	Excellent Poor
Healthy eating message	1 ←————————————————→ 5
	Excellent Poor
Colourful	1 ←————————————————→ 5
	Excellent Poor
Attractive to the customer	1 ←————————————————→ 5
	Excellent Poor

Compare your ratings with the table about your skills that you completed in Task 1.

- English – reading and interpreting instructions.
- CDT – drawing up patterns.
- Art and Design – could help you with colour choices.

TASK 1

In pairs, design a uniform for the front-of-house staff of the Healthy Eating bistro.

a. Draw out your design and detail the colours you would use for each part of the design.

b. Make a list of all the fabric properties the uniform must have.

c. Draw out a care label for the uniform.

TASK 2

Design a logo that could be embroidered on to chefs' whites at the Healthy Eating bistro.

TASK 3

Chefs' whites must be made from fabric that is non-flammable. Chefs also require steel toe-capped, non-slip footwear.

Other types of occupations also require safety clothing. Research one of the following occupations and identify all the safety clothing and footwear that would be required.

- fireman
- nurse
- surgeon
- policeman
- painter and decorator
- construction worker
- mountain rescue worker
- lifeboat crew

If time allows, draw a picture of the safety clothing and footwear required.

MY LEARNING CHECKLIST

Put a tick in the column to show how you think you got
on with each statement on your Learning Checklist.

Green means you got on really well with your learning in this area.
Amber means you did well with your learning.
Red means you need to do a bit of work on your learning.

Good to go!   *Getting there*   *Help needed*

1. **I am able to follow instructions to make a keyring.**

2. **I am able to use a range of sewing equipment and a sewing machine safely.**

3. **I know the fabric properties needed for my school sports kit and how to care for it.**

4. **I am aware of the safety requirements needed in clothing for certain occupations.**

5. **I am able to promote a healthy eating message through a textile design.**

PERSONAL REVIEW

Knowing how to apply basic fabric skills to design is important in my everyday life because: _____

Being aware of fabric properties will help when selecting fabrics for a range of purposes because: _____

AFTER COMPLETING THIS CHAPTER WHAT DO YOU FEEL YOU HAVE GAINED MORE CONFIDENCE IN DOING?

I feel more **confident** in: _____

84

THINK-PAIR-SHARE

- On your own, think about each of the statements on the sheet and complete each box.
- With a partner, exchange answers.
- Both of you will then share your answers with other pairs or the whole class.

QUESTION OR PROMPT	WHAT I THOUGHT	WHAT MY PARTNER THOUGHT	WHAT WE WILL SHARE
Why is care labelling important?			
What is the most important fabric property of your school uniform?			

My name: _____

Partner's name: _____

Date: _____

DESIGN AND THE CHALLENGES IT BRINGS

Whether it's a new sewing machine, pair of jeans or new food product that is being designed, the following basic principles apply.

The ABC of design

A – Analyse
Analyse the given design brief and list all the factors (points) that need to be considered for the design.

B – Brainstorm
Brainstorm each factor, and from this identify specific design features that must be included in the final design.

C – Create
Using the design features you have identified, create a design specification.

A + B = C

A

Many factors have to be considered before starting to design.
- Cost
- Safety
- Likes/dislikes
- Function
- Resources
- Environmental concerns
- Health issues
- Lifestyle needs
- Target group

The above factors are examples. There are many other factors that could be considered.

B

From these factors, the following are examples of how design features are expanded to meet the needs of the target group.
- Cost to buy, cost to produce
- Food safety, safety in use
- Appearance, colour, texture, taste
- What it is going to be used for
- Equipment/materials available, practical skills
- Recycling, food miles
- Allergies, diet-related diseases, e.g. heart disease, obesity
- Time and energy savings, cultural needs
- Age, level of activity, disabilities

The above features often link to more than one factor, e.g. health issues and suitability for target group.

C

The design specification must link to both A and B.

E.g. a low-fat cook-chill meal for an obese adult must be low in fat and taste good (health features linked to likes and dislikes).

E.g. baby clothing should have no buttons or sharp fastenings (safety features linked to suitability for target group).

THE NEXT 5 STEPS IN THE DESIGN CHALLANGE

1. Using the design specification(C), come up with a range of possible design ideas by drawing sketches by hand, or by using an ICT package such as CAD (Computer Aided Design).
2. Evaluate all the possible design ideas generated and decide which one to take forward.
3. Make a sample (known as a prototype) of your design and get the target group to trial it.
4. Evaluate the results of the trial and make any changes to the design.
5. Put your final solution into production.

ACTIVITIES

TASK 1

Working in pairs, conduct some market research in order to create a questionnaire of six questions that will be handed out to the class to find out their opinions on the lunch provision in school.

Collate the results and evaluate your findings.

TASK 2

Identify and explain four specific design features you would have to consider when designing the following items.
- A feeding dish for a toddler.
- A set of new pans for the elderly.
- A new case for carrying a piece of portable IT equipment.

TASK 3

Food waste is a growing concern. Supermarkets are aware that some foods with limited shelf lives are reduced in price at the end of the day in order to meet with

food safety regulations. Come up with a creative recipe that uses this food.

a. Identify a food that is often reduced at the end of the day.
b. Analyse all the factors that would need to be considered, e.g. other foods available, skills, target group.
c. Brainstorm each factor and make a list of the design features needed for the recipe.
d. Devise a five-point specification for the recipe.

If you have time, trial out some of the recipe suggestions as a class.

MAKE THE LINK

CDT – designing and making a variety of items to suit a purpose using different materials.

Enterprise Activity – designing a product to raise funds, e.g. for a charity.

Art and Design – sketching design ideas.

Business Education – designing market research questionnaires.

DID YOU KNOW?

Designing is like a chain reaction, one link leads to another, e.g. the development of microwaves has led to the introduction of microwavable meals, which has led to the need for microwavable packaging. The next link in this chain was the development of freezer-to-microwave meals and packaging.

87

OUR EVERYDAY LIVES

Products are constantly being developed or updated for a variety of reasons such as changes in market trends (e.g. food-to-go ranges/simply food), competition from other manufacturers and advances in technology (e.g. new developments in kitchen equipment). Manufacturers use market research to find out what consumers want. This can be done through questionnaires, interviews and supermarket surveys. ICT packages are used to collate the results.

TOP TIP
To prevent opinions being influenced, it is important that the target groups do not communicate with each other when trialling the prototype.

THE CHALLENGE!

A manufacturer has come up with the following design brief.

Design a Smart Start range of cook–chill savoury products to be used when weaning a baby.

The following is an example of how to use the ABC of design to develop a suitable product for the range.

CHALLENGE

Ⓐ Analyse the design brief and identify the factors (points) that need to be considered.

- Cost
- Safety
- Likes/dislikes
- Resources
- Health issues
- Suitability for target group

Ⓑ Brainstorm each factor and, from this, identify specific design features that must be included in the final design. Present each factor as a mind map.

- Cost: affordable to buy, value for money.
- Safety: food safety – heating instructions, storage instructions, easy to eat (no hard ingredients/choking hazards/puréed).
- Likes/dislikes: taste/flavour, appearance, smell, consistency, variety.
- Resources: cooking equipment, suitable foods available, practical skills, production time, reheating time, methods of reheating, storage equipment.
- Health issues: allergies, e.g. no nuts, no strong flavours, no fat, salt levels.
- Target group: nutritional content, e.g. calcium, protein; 4–6 months, products already on the market.

Ⓒ Create a five-point design specification using the information from the brainstorming. The product should:

- Be affordable for parents to buy (cost).
- Have clear reheating instructions (safety).
- Have a good flavour without adding salt (likes/dislikes and health issues).
- Be suitable for a cook–chill range (resources).
- Contain a range of nutrients (target group).

Step 1
Using the design specification come up with a range of possible design ideas. Possible ideas – pasta bolognese, puréed chicken with sweet potato, one-pot chicken and vegetable hot pot, curried chicken and boiled rice, beef cottage pie.

Step 2
Evaluate all the possible design ideas against the specification and decide which one to take forward to the next stage.

- Spaghetti bolognese – not suitable as spaghetti is choke hazard.
- Puréed chicken with sweet potato – suitable as it offers a variety of flavours and is easy to eat.
- One-pot chicken and vegetable hot pot – not suitable as dish contains chunky bits of vegetable.
- Curried chicken and boiled rice – not suitable as it is too spicy and rice is a choke hazard.
- Beef cottage pie – suitable if the beef is finely puréed.

Step 3
Make a sample (known as a prototype) of your design and get the target group to trial it.

Step 4
Evaluate the results of the trial and make any changes to the design. The product was trialled by a group of mothers and their babies from the local 'Buggy' group.

Results: The product tasted good and was well received by the mothers, as it was easy to prepare. All the babies ate it, which showed that they liked it. Some mothers said they would have liked it to contain more vegetables.

Step 5
Put your final solution into production.

ACTIVITIES

TASK 1

Working in pairs, complete the following stages in this small design challenge. You are considering starting a cup cake business from home and have to design a suitable topping for your cup cakes.

Step 1

1. Decide on a target group for your cup cakes.
2. Brainstorm possible themes for the cup cakes.
3. Propose two possible designs for the cup cake topping and decide on one.

Step 2

4. Make the cup cakes using the basic recipe below.

   Ingredients

125g soft margarine	2 medium eggs
125g caster sugar	2 tablespoons milk
125g self-raising flour	12-hole muffin tins, lined with paper cases

   Method

   1. Heat oven to 190°C or Gas Mark 5.
   2. Place all the ingredients in a large bowl and whisk with an electric mixer for five minutes until light and fluffy.
   3. Divide the mixture between all the paper cases and bake for 15–20 minutes until a light golden colour.
   4. Cool the cup cakes (**you may have to freeze them for the next lesson**).

Step 3

5. Decorate with your chosen design and photograph one of your cakes. Your class could then vote for the best cup cake.

Step 4

6. Evaluate your topping, linked to your theme and target group.

TASK 2

Develop a wordsearch to include ten words linked to the A B C of design.

TOP TIP
To help prevent obesity only feed babies two or three teaspoonfuls of solids when they start weaning.

MAKE THE LINK

Art and Design – developing creativity in designs.

ICT – refining web research skills.

DID YOU KNOW?

Many of our products have been developed to suit our lifestyle needs, e.g. convenience foods that have short prepration times and require little skill to prepare. However, because of foreign travel, cultural interests and environmental concerns there is an increasing demand for a wider range of food products. This unfortunately has resulted in an increase in the distance food travels before it lands on your plate (food miles). Consumers are becoming less aware of when foods are in season.

OUR EVERYDAY LIVES

When manufacturers or restaurants develop a new product, they have to consider the sustainability of the ingredients they include (i.e. ingredients being available all year round). The importation of foods has helped with this but it has also resulted in increased costs and enlarged carbon footprints.

TASK 3

Work in pairs to complete the **Student Challenge**. When teenagers leave school and study away from home, they have to take more responsibility for looking after their health. There is a greater risk of becoming overweight through unhealthy snacking or not taking the time to cook proper meals due to their busy lifestyles.

Develop a healthy one-pot meal suitable for a student who is living in a hall of residence where they share a kitchen with other students.

INTERDISCIPLINARY PROJECT

DESIGN CHALLENGE

Primary 7 pupils will soon have an S1 Induction Day at your school. You have been asked to:

'Develop a new health-promoting main course or dessert to encourage S1 pupils to use the school canteen.'

TASK 1

a. Working in groups, carry out some research into the foods already served in the school canteen. You could do this through:
   - looking at the menus to find out what is already on offer.
   - giving questionnaires to pupils to see which foods are popular (market research).
   You may wish to find out about any nutritional guidelines the school canteen has to follow.

b. Analyse the design brief and decide on the important factors that need to be considered.
   Brainstorm these factors and list the design features that the product will need.
   Create a five-point specification for the product.

c. Using the design specification, come up with a range of possible design ideas. This can be done by drawing sketches by hand, or by using an IT program.

d. Evaluate all the possible design ideas generated and decide which one to take forward to the next stage.

e. Make a sample (known as a prototype) of your design and photograph it.
   Make up a sensory evaluation sheet and use this to trial out your product with some S1 pupils.

f. Evaluate the results of the trial and make any changes to the design.

g. Present your final copy of the recipe along with your photograph.

h. Design a set of symbols for the canteen to use beside their menu to show if the dishes are low in fat, low in salt, low in sugar or high in dietary fibre.

MAKE THE LINK

- Art and Design – design symbols for the menu.
- Business Education – design and collate the questionnaires.
- CDT – application of a specification.

ACTIVITIES

TASK 1

a. In pairs, design a 'cartoon of the term' to promote the use of the school canteen.

b. The class should be divided into four groups. Each group should take one of the following times in the school year and come up with a series of cartoons for that school term.
   - Summer to October (Autumn term)
   - October to December (Winter term)
   - January to March (Spring term)
   - April to June (Summer term)

Remember to consider the foods in season and the type of climate that could affect food choice.

Make your cartoons fun!

The cartoons could be displayed around the school.

TASK 2

On your own, design a cover for a school planner to be used by the new S1 pupils. The design should encourage:
- smart food choices
- a healthy lifestyle.

You could include some **Top Tips** for good health in your design.

TASK 3

Go to www.mapsofworld.com and download a world map.

The ingredients for a risotto include: baby courgettes, sweetcorn, chicken, peppers, carrot, onion, and risotto rice.

- Carry out some research, either at the supermarket or using websites, to find out where these ingredients come from.
- Draw lines on your world map showing where these foods have travelled from to where you live.
- Try to work out the food miles that each food has travelled.
- Which food travelled furthest?
- What is the total mileage of your risotto?

91

MY LEARNING CHECKLIST

Put a tick in the column to show how you think you got on with
each statement on your Learning Checklist.

Green means you got on really well with your learning in this area.
Amber means you did well with your learning.
Red means you need to do a bit of work on your learning.

	Good to go!	Getting there	Help needed
1. I can work my way through the ABC of design.	◯	◯	◯
2. I can write a five-point specification.	◯	◯	◯
3. I understand the meaning of the term 'prototype'.	◯	◯	◯
4. I can produce a solution to a design brief.	◯	◯	◯
5. I have developed evaluation skills.	◯	◯	◯

PERSONAL REVIEW

Knowing that design features will vary according to people's needs will help me
in my everyday life because: _____

Knowing how to apply my evaluation skills will help me in my future life because:

_____

**AFTER WORKING IN A TEAM FOR THE DESIGN CHALLENGE DO YOU FEEL YOU HAVE
CONTRIBUTED EFFECTIVELY ?**

I think I **contributed effectively** because: _____

92

THINK-PAIR-SHARE

- On your own think about each of the statements on the sheet and complete each box.
- Exchange answers with a partner.
- Both of you will then share your answers with other pairs or the whole class.

QUESTION OR PROMPT	WHAT I THOUGHT	WHAT MY PARTNER THOUGHT	WHAT WE WILL SHARE
Should manufacturers consider food miles when designing a new food product?			
Discuss the most important design features for a can opener that is to be used by someone who has a disability.			

My name: _____

Partner's name: _____

Date: _____

THE SMART COOK
PAGE 13
Task 1

Basic Technique	Description	Equipment required
Peel	The process of removing the outer skin from fruit or vegetables.	Vegetable knife Vegetable peeler
Cut	The process of breaking the surface of a food to divide or make it smaller.	Cook's knife Vegetable knife Chopping board
Slice	To cut across a food item, making it into thin pieces that are similar in thickness.	Cook's knife Vegetable knife Electric food processor
Grate	To make food into smaller pieces or shreds by rubbing it against a grating surface.	All purpose grater Rotary grater Electric food processor
Rub in	To rub fat into flour using the fingertips. The flour particles are coated with the fat and the mixture resembles breadcrumbs, e.g. pastry making.	Round bladed knife Electric food processor
Mix	To combine ingredients so that they are all distributed evenly within the mixture.	Fork Whisks Food processor
Whisk	To mix ingredients together or to add air into ingredients to increase the volume, e.g. whisking cream.	Hand held electric whisk, rotary, balloon or flat whisk
Cream	To beat margarine and caster sugar together until the mixture is light and fluffy, e.g. cake making.	Wooden spoon and mixing bowl Hand held electric whisk Electric food processor
Blend	To mix together a dry ingredient with a liquid to give a smooth paste, e.g. blending custard powder with milk.	Wooden spoon Balloon Whisk Flat Whisk Teaspoon
Roll out	To make pastry or dough thinner and smoother before it is shaped.	Rolling pin Flour dredger
Shape	To take food ingredients and form them into an appropriate shape, e.g. beef burgers, scones.	Palette knife Pastry cutters

94

Task 2

Macédoine – Small cubed dice either
3×3×3mm or 5×5×5mm

Jardinière – Batons either 3×3×18mm or
5×5×15mm

Paysanne – thin flat cut of triangles, squares
or rounds 1 cm in size

BEAT THE 'G' TEAM
PAGE 27
Task 2

a. Prawns, seafood sauce, chicken,
   mayonnaise, cooked rice
b. Hygiene controls could include:

Personal hygiene

Any example of personal hygiene during
preparation or serving, e.g. washing hands
before handling foods, tying hair back,
wearing clean apron etc.

Storage

Store all high risk foods in a refrigerator
before/after preparation.
Temperature of the refrigerator should be
4°C or less.
Refrigerator should not be overloaded.
Store raw chicken in a separate refrigerator.
Food should be covered in a refrigerator.
Cooked food should be stored above raw
chicken.
Rice, after cooking, should be stored in the
fridge for as short a time as possible.

Preparation

Separate boards/preparation areas for
raw foods.
Foods should be in the danger zone/
warm area of the kitchen for the minimum
amount of time.

Cooking

After cooking, the rice/chicken should be
quickly cooled and then refrigerated
Chicken should be thoroughly cooked – no
pink areas.

Serving

The length of time food sits out after being
served should be minimal/no longer than
30 minutes.

BEAT THE 'G' TEAM
PAGE 27
Task 3

1 – a   2 – d   3 – b   4 – c

ALL IN THE PROCESS
PAGE 33
Task 3

Dietary Target Sudoku Solution

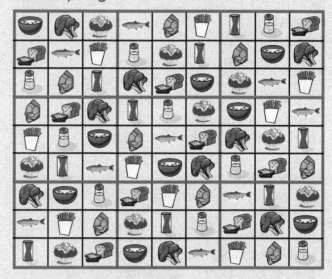

GETTING IT RIGHT
PAGE 43
Task 2

Healthy Hannah

Your letter could include the following
points:

1. • Choose low fat versions of products like
     milk, yoghurt, spreads
   • Eat foods that are good sources of
     fibre – these are more filling and will
     reduce the temptation to snack on
     sugary, fatty treats
   • Eat less sugary/fatty foods
   • Eat plenty of fruit and vegetables
   • Avoid snacking between meals or eat
     fruit as snacks
   • Read the labels on processed foods as
     they often contain a lot of sugars and
     fats
   • Eat a balanced diet with 3 meals – this
     should stop her feeling hungry
   • Reduce the size of portion served.
   • Take regular, gentle exercise.

ANSWERS

2. • Eat wholegrain products like
    wholemeal bread, wholegrain
    breakfast cereals
  • Eat plenty of fruit and vegetables/
    5 portions daily, including the skins
  • Add extra vegetables to stews, etc.
  • Drink plenty of water.

GETTING IT RIGHT
PAGE 47
Task 2

Fat per serving
KFC Hot and Spicy Chicken Thighs 28g
Subway Spicy Italian 6-inch sub 25g
Starbucks chocolate-filled croissant 19g
McDonalds Quarter Pounder 19g

Sodium per serving
Subway Honey Mustard Ham 6-inch sub
1410mg
KFC Hot Wings 1120mg
McDonalds Big Mac 1050mg
Burger King Dutch Apple Tart 470mg

Sugar per serving
McDonald's Hot Caramel Sundae 47g
Burger King fresh-baked cookies 32g
Starbucks blueberry muffin 28g
KFC Apple Pie Slice 22g
Source www.fastfoodfacts.info

GETTING IT RIGHT
PAGE 49
Task 2

Your letter could include the following points:
High blood pressure
  • When your heart beats, it pumps blood
    round your body to give it the energy and
    oxygen it needs.
  • Thickening and hardening of artery walls
    will cause the heart to work harder. This
    causes blood pressure to rise as the heart
    tries to pump the blood round your body.
  • If your blood pressure is too high, it puts
    extra strain on your arteries (and your
    heart) and this may lead to heart attacks
    and strokes in later life.

Teenagers
  • Avoid eating salty snacks and foods.
  • Taste your food before adding salt.
  • Do not eat too many processed/fast
    foods as they may contain a lot of salt.
  • Read the label on foods to check the salt
    content.
  • Do not become overweight.
  • Exercise regularly.
  • Avoid drinking too much alcohol.
  • Do not smoke.

GETTING IT RIGHT FOR ALL
PAGE 57
Task 2

Practical ways could include:
  • Wholegrain breakfast cereal/porridge in
    the morning
  • Sandwiches using wholemeal bread/rolls
  • Bananas
  • Rice dishes, e.g. savoury rice (preferably
    wholegrain)
  • Pasta dishes, e.g. pasta and tomato
    sauce (preferably wholegrain)
  • Baked potatoes and a filling
  • Soups that contain pulses.

GETTING IT RIGHT FOR ALL
PAGE 59
Task 2

You could make the following changes:
  • Minced beef to Quorn
  • Beef stock to vegetable stock
  • Butter to vegetable oil based margarine,
    e.g. sunflower oil or olive oil / soya
    margarine
  • Milk to soya milk

GETTING IT RIGHT FOR ALL
PAGE 63
Task 2

1 – sports person, diabetic, teenager,
    toddler
2 – person with an allergy, toddlers
3 – vegan vegetarian
4 – pregnant woman, convalescent,
    elderly, any of the groups trying to
    reduce weight
5 – pregnant woman, teenager, elderly, any
    of the groups suffering from anaemia

6 – diabetic, toddlers, any of the groups trying to reduce weight

7 – elderly, pregnant women, any of the groups suffering from bowel disorders

8 – Lacto-ovo vegetarian
Other examples are acceptable if you can give a correct reason for your answer

PACKAGING MATTERS
PAGE 67
Task 1
Concerns could include:

Packaging matters	Concerns Consumer (C) Manufacturer (M) Retailer (R)
Glass	Could smash if dropped so may cause injury (C) Heavy to carry home (C) Shape can make them difficult to stack on a shelf (R)
Aluminium/steel	Uses a lot of energy/raw materials during production (M) Many people do not recycle these so adds to landfill sites (M)
Paper	Very easily torn/damaged/not waterproof (C)
Cardboard	Can be bulky to store (R) Can be easily damaged/not waterproof (R)
Tetra packs	Can be difficult to recycle (M) Can be difficult to open (C)
Plastic	Some may not be microwaveable and could be damaged in the microwave (C) Can fill up/contaminate landfill sites if not biodegradable(M) Some types take a long time to degrade (M) Some shapes are difficult to store (R)
Modified atmosphere packaging	Food starts to deteriorate once the package is opened so doesn't last long (C)
Vacuum packaging	Packaging is sometimes difficult to recycle(M) Can be difficult to open (C)

PACKAGING MATTERS
PAGE 67
Task 4

Packaging	Advantages	Disadvantages
Tetra packs	Can be bought in single portions so useful for packed lunches Strong Lightweight to carry	Difficult to recycle Difficult for consumer to open
Glass	Contents can be seen Easy to recycle Re-usable for consumer	Heavy to carry Easily broken May be more expensive to buy
Plastic	Strong Lightweight to carry May be cheaper to buy Non-breakable	Some types cannot be recycled

97

ANSWERS

PACKAGING MATTERS
PAGE 69
Task 2

1. "e" means the average weight of the product. Some may weigh slightly more, some slightly less.

2. Most fresh vegetables – Soup A as it contains 42% carrots and 7% onion (49% fresh vegetables in total). Soup B has a total of 38% fresh vegetables.

   Most saturated fat – Soup B as it contains double cream. The other soup does not state what kind of cream it contains.

   Most salt – Soup B as both salt and vegetable bouillon are included on its ingredients list.

3. Soup A

4. Leftover soup can be frozen and used later because the quality will be unaffected by freezing.

   Good for students/people living on their own as it prevents wastage.

5. A non-metallic container will not taint/affect the flavour of the soup.

   It will also be safe to reheat the soup in a microwave in a non-metallic container. Refrigeration prevents bacteria multiplying.

6. Soup B would be useful as an emergency standby because tins can be stored for a long time.

NTERDISCIPLINARY PROJECT: THE WHOLE PACKAGE

AGE 75

Task 1

Tricky Crossword Puzzle

1	2	3	4	5	6	7	8	9	10	11	12	13	14	15	16	17	18	19	20	21	22	23	24	25	26
Z	Y	T	F	U	A	I	C	G	S	O	J	L	X	E	R	W	Q	B	K	P	H	D	N	V	M

B 19	O 11	I 7	L 13	S 10		C 8	O 11	O 11	K 20	I 7	N 24	G 9	
A 6								X 14					
C 8	L 13	E 15	A 6	N 24			H 22	Y 2	G 9	I 7	E 15	N 24	E 15
T 3		H 22						G 9					
E 15		O 11		S 10				E 15				W 17	
R 16			S 10	A 6	L 13	M 26	O 11	N 24	E 15	L 13	L 13	A 6	
I 7	L 13	L 13		L 13		O 11						R 16	
A 6				T 3		I 7				T 3	I 7	M 26	E 15
	D 23					S 10						T 3	
	E 15		L 13	I 7	S 10	T 3	E 15	R 16	I 7	A 6		H 22	
	F 4					U 5		E 15					
	R 16	I 7	C 8	E 15		R 16		H 22		M 26	E 15	A 6	T 3
	O 11					E 15		E 15					H 22
	S 10							A 6					A 6
	T 3	E 15	M 26	P 21	E 15	R 16	A 6	T 3	U 5	R 16	E 15		W 17

ANSWERS

Task 3

Food	Packaging	Reason
Soup for the freezer	Rigid plastic container Strong, resealable plastic freezer bag	Will prevent soup becoming affected by the low temperature/freezer burn Rigid plastic container will not allow soup to leak or burst Freezer bag may take up less space in the freezer
Raw meat	Plastic bag Tin foil Plastic container	Will ensure that blood does not leak from the raw meat and contaminate other foods
Fatless sponge cake	Airtight container	Keeps the air out which would make the sponge go hard

DESIGN AND THE CHALLENGES IT BRINGS
Task 2

Any four design features from the following list:

	Design feature	Explanation
Feeding dish for toddler	Stable base Outside does not heat up but inside keeps food warm Attractive/colourful Dishwasher proof	So it is not easily knocked over by the toddler So the toddler does not get burned but food is warm to eat To encourage the toddler to eat To make sure it is clean and hygienic
Pans for the elderly	Lightweight Handle does not heat up A spout on one of the pans Easy to clean Pans should be stackable	Elderly may have difficulty lifting Prevents elderly person burning their fingers/hand when lifting Helps the elderly person to pour, e.g. soup Saves the elderly person effort Saves space as the elderly person may have a small storage area/kitchen
Carrying case	Strong material used for the case Strong handle Lockable	To protect the IT equipment from damage The IT equipment may be heavy to carry To make it more secure